# NETWORKING

## An Electronic Mail Handbook

Thomas B. Cross         Marjorie B. Raizman

Scott, Foresman and Company

Glenview, Illinois         London

*To William and Bonnie Spencer*

For their determination in pioneering new means of communication

ISBN 0-673-18008-5

Copyright © 1986 Scott, Foresman and Company.
All Rights Reserved.
Printed in the United States of America.

**Library of Congress Cataloging-in-Publication Data**

Cross, Thomas B.
  Networking: an electronic mail handbook.

  Bibliography: p. 207.
  Includes index.
  1. Electronic mail systems.   I. Raizman, Marjorie B.
II. Title.
HE6239.E54C76   1985        384.1'4        85-22136
ISBN 0-673-18008-5

1 2 3 4 5 6KPF-90 89 88 87 86 85

Pp. 17-18: Discussion from Desmond Smith, "The Wiring of Wall St.," *New York Times Magazine*, October 23, 1983, p. 44 f. Copyright © by The New York Times Company. Reprinted by permission.

Pp. 19-20, 167, 169: Discussion from Kathleen Wiegner and Ellen Paris, "A Job with a View," *Forbes*, September 12, 1983, pp. 143-150. Used with permission of the publisher.

Fig. 1.2 adapted by permission of Management Technology. Fig. 3.3 reprinted by permission of NBI, Inc. Fig. 4.3 reprinted by permission of ROLM® Corporation. Fig. 4.5 reprinted by permission of DEST Corporation. Fig. 4.7 reprinted by permission of Digital Sound Corporation, Santa Barbara, CA.

Notice of Liability
The information in this book is distributed on an "As Is" basis, without warranty. Neither the author nor Scott, Foresman and Company shall have any liability to customer or any other person or entity with respect to any liability, loss, or damage caused or alleged to be caused directly or indirectly by the programs contained herein. This includes, but is not limited to, interruption of service, loss of data, loss of business or anticipatory profits, or consequential damages from the use of the programs.

# Preface

In developing new means of communication, we are often faced with the problem of getting the message across. Sometimes the message will be more important than the messenger, but it is often the other way around. We have written this book as an introduction to the messages and the messengers. From that vantage point, you can then develop your own approach to this exciting and important technology.

## Acknowledgments

We would like to thank Alan W. Harris, Andrew McKay, Daniel C. Thomann, and Ronald Kauffman for their inspiration and guidance.

We would also like to thank Kathleen Kelleher and Marc Raizman for their editorial guidance, as well as Warren Kirk and Saundra L. Carmical for their assistance in preparing the graphics.

THOMAS B. CROSS
MARJORIE B. RAIZMAN

# Contents

## PART ONE   Overview

## PART TWO   Electronic Mail Operations

# PART THREE Integrating Electronic Mail Successfully

# PART ONE

# Overview

What is electronic mail? Who uses it? What are some successful applications of electronic mail? How did it develop? What are future trends in electronic mail?

# 1 Electronic Mail: An Introduction

## WHAT IS ELECTRONIC MAIL (EM)?

Electronic mail (EM) is an electronic communications system that is used to send information from one person/site to another (one-to-one communication), or from one person to many people at the same time (called broadcasting or one-to-many communications). Depending on the system used, electronic messages can comprise data, text, audio, or graphic information. However, unlike regular letters that are written on paper and sent via the postal service, "electronic letters" and "electronic packages" are entered into a terminal and then transmitted electronically, arriving almost instantaneously instead of taking a day or more to reach their destination.

Electronic mail facilitates communications and information exchange in a multitude of ways and touches every aspect of the communications industry (see Figure 1.1). EM is used by salespeople scattered across the country (or around the world) to ask questions of the home office or to submit orders for products. It enables medical personnel in remote areas to consult with experts located at central medical facilities. Students at Dartmouth hand in their homework via EM. The White House, Cabinet members, and certain government department staffs send messages via the Executive Data Link EM system, a service that covers about 100 electronic mailboxes.[1] Technically advanced EM systems provide common files and a direct communications link for people who are working together on a project, yet are dispersed throughout an organization. They also provide users with the means to track projects, centralize or decentralize business tasks, educate, telecommute, and teleconference.

3

## FIGURE 1.1

Electronic mail touches every aspect of the communications industry.

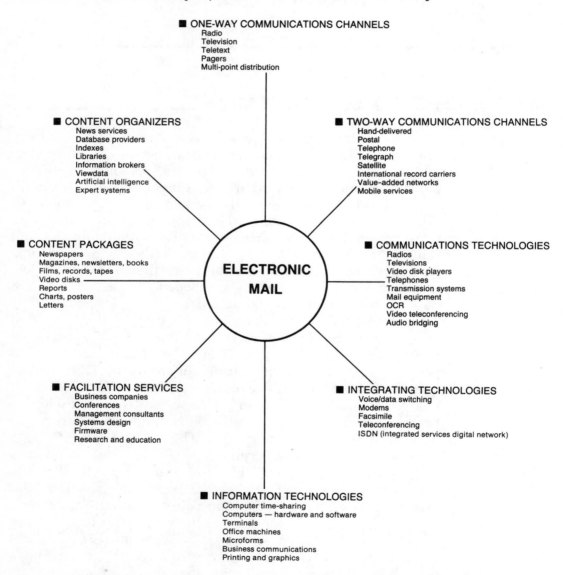

■ ONE-WAY COMMUNICATIONS CHANNELS
Radio
Television
Teletext
Pagers
Multi-point distribution

■ CONTENT ORGANIZERS
News services
Database providers
Indexes
Libraries
Information brokers
Viewdata
Artificial intelligence
Expert systems

■ TWO-WAY COMMUNICATIONS CHANNELS
Hand-delivered
Postal
Telephone
Telegraph
Satellite
International record carriers
Value-added networks
Mobile services

■ CONTENT PACKAGES
Newspapers
Magazines, newsletters, books
Films, records, tapes
Video disks
Reports
Charts, posters
Letters

**ELECTRONIC MAIL**

■ COMMUNICATIONS TECHNOLOGIES
Radios
Televisions
Video disk players
Telephones
Transmission systems
Mail equipment
OCR
Video teleconferencing
Audio bridging

■ FACILITATION SERVICES
Business companies
Conferences
Management consultants
Systems design
Firmware
Research and education

■ INTEGRATING TECHNOLOGIES
Voice/data switching
Modems
Facsimile
Teleconferencing
ISDN (integrated services digital network)

■ INFORMATION TECHNOLOGIES
Computer time-sharing
Computers — hardware and software
Terminals
Office machines
Microforms
Business communications
Printing and graphics

Use of EM systems has grown exponentially in the last ten years, with about one billion electronic messages sent in 1984. Analysts predict that that number will increase to 4 billion by 1988, 19 billion by 1990, and 60 billion by the year 2000.[2] The proliferation of organizations that use electronic mail and of newsletters that write about it attests to the growing acceptance of this way of communicating.

# EM REPLACES TELEPHONE AND POSTAL SERVICES

Electronic mail can replace most communications that transmit simple items of information. Some observers question the reliability of the United States Postal Service in doing so. Columnist William F. Buckley, Jr., describes an experiment in which 363 New York City executives mailed each other first-class letters during July 1983: "Forty-two of those [letters] arrived the following day . . . and 21 percent [of them] never arrived at all," according to Buckley.[3] He predicts that eventually "the principal use of the computer" will be to carry out communication.

The *New York Times* speculates that, because 50 percent of first-class mail consists of billings or payments which "are being handled more and more frequently by computerized electronic networks," the regular postal service may be "headed for extinction" unless it is able to plug into the electronic age.[4]

Electronic mail has several advantages over traditional mail and/or telephone messages. Traditional mail is one-way communication in which a person sends a message without being able to interact with the recipient. Because electronic messages are transmitted almost instantaneously, electronic mail can effectively become two-way communication, allowing sender and recipient to interact as they attempt to resolve problems or make decisions.

Another advantage of electronic mail over traditional mail is that "the message always goes through," whereas letters are not delivered by the Postal Service on Sundays or holidays or during postal strikes, and may not be delivered in severe weather. International mail is even more of a problem, letters often taking weeks to arrive and sometimes not arriving at all.

There are several disadvantages to using the telephone to communicate. Studies have found that business telephone calls are completed only about one-third of the time because those who are called are unavailable. When calls are long-distance, expensive "telephone tag" results—and as the number of time zones increases, so does the chance for telephone tag. In addition, the telephone is a poor medium for lengthy, accurate transmission of information. In order to ensure that participants have clearly understood each other, important conversations must be confirmed in writing. This requires secretarial labor and mailing time, as well as paper and postage.

## EM: THE NEW WAY TO COMMUNICATE

A major difference between electronic messaging systems today and those of yesterday is that current systems do not require the sender and recipient to be on-line simultaneously. More advanced equipment, such as communicating word processors and personal computers, allows users to communicate when they choose, in a "store-and-forward" or asynchronous mode.

Store-and-forward means that messages are placed in the system at the sender's convenience and held for transmission at a given time. This may be when transmission rates are lower or when a network becomes available. Messages are then forwarded when the recipient requests delivery. In addition, modern systems operate faster than early ones and provide better-quality printing.

Electronic mail also performs a multitude of other functions, including the following:

- Enables communication to take place regardless of the geographical locations/time zones of the sender/recipient, weather conditions, holidays, and postal strikes.
- Cuts messaging time, whether the sender communicates with one person or "broadcasts" to many people and/or locations at the same time.

- Holds messages until the sender requests transmission, then stores them in the addressee's EM box until they are called up on a monitor or ordered to be printed.
- Establishes message or information files.
- Records messages automatically and accurately.
- Tracks messages systematically and establishes a message "audit trail."
- Allows users to annotate and forward messages and files.
- Enables users to edit textual material while preparing messages.
- Allows users to connect electronically with other networks.

# HOW EM HELPS BUSINESSES

## EM Upgrades Communications

Electronic mail upgrades the quality of communication in a number of ways, often enabling it to take place in situations where it was not previously possible. For example, when company personnel must travel, they are able to send messages electronically by accessing portable company computers which they connect to ordinary telephones. Thus they can travel to remote locations without losing touch with the home office. An organization's communication process is also upgraded because messages can be quickly answered. For example, the head of a police department found that he can dispose of 75 incoming messages within one-and-a-half hours using EM.[5] Electronic mail also encourages the use of informal/friendly language that helps to bridge social barriers.[6] In addition, it:

- Permits managers to log onto a system and track information that has been entered concerning a project.
- Supports activities such as conferencing. For example, information can be exchanged and questions can be handled before meetings, thus eliminating the need to discuss meeting agendas and formats.
- Informs and reminds users of scheduled events.

- Reduces message reading time because EM users generally express themselves concisely.
- Increases the scope of information and communications flow, allowing more people, expertise, and data to be included.

## EM Saves Time and Reduces Costs

In companies that use electronic mail, the time that managers and professionals spend in communications-related activities is significantly reduced. An AT&T study pegs the time that a manager/professional spends in these activities at about 94 percent of the working day.[7] Another study, carried out in 1984 by Cross Information Company of Boulder, Colorado, analyzed the average manager's distribution of working hours and forecasts their future time distribution as follows:

**Present**
- Meetings ....................................... 30%
- Telephone  .................................... 20%
- Travel ......................................... 20%
- Information search/transactions/desk work ..... 30%

**Future**
- Communications/information transactions, meetings, presentations, audio and video conferencing  .... 40%
- Travel  ....................................... 10%
- Seeking information/transactions, dictation, telephone, computer conferencing, viewdata (interactive informational systems), decision support systems (assisted "thinking"), computer-assisted retrieval ......... 50%

A study carried out by Manufacturers Hanover Trust, the fourth-largest U.S. commercial bank, found that EM saved 3,000 of its employees about 36 minutes each day (see Figure 1.2). This amounted to a savings for the bank of about $7 million in 1982.[8] Secretaries working for the United Service Auto Association (USAA), a major insurance carrier with a large-scale in-house EM system, found that EM increased their productivity by 50 percent and reduced the flow of interoffice memos by 10 percent.[9]

## FIGURE 1.2

Time saved each day by electronic mail users at Manufacturers Hanover Trust.

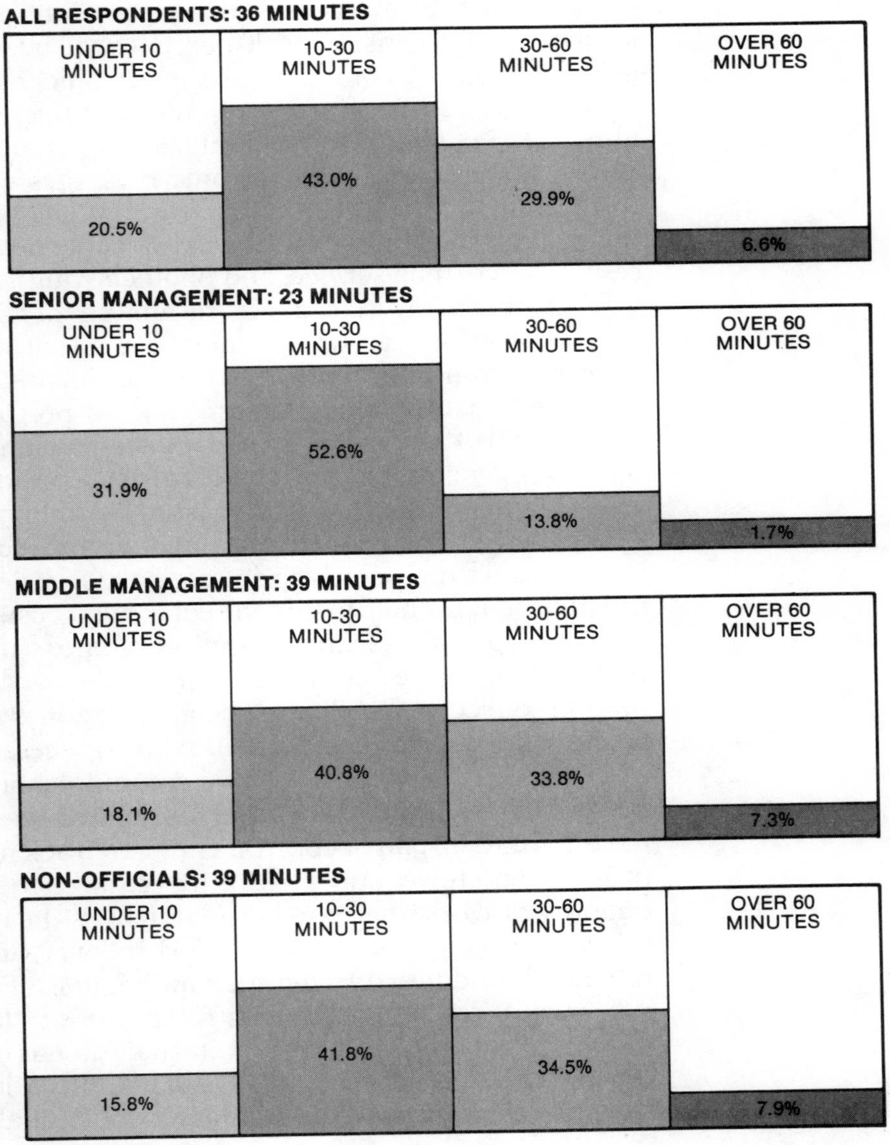

**ALL RESPONDENTS: 36 MINUTES**

| UNDER 10 MINUTES | 10-30 MINUTES | 30-60 MINUTES | OVER 60 MINUTES |
|---|---|---|---|
| 20.5% | 43.0% | 29.9% | 6.6% |

**SENIOR MANAGEMENT: 23 MINUTES**

| UNDER 10 MINUTES | 10-30 MINUTES | 30-60 MINUTES | OVER 60 MINUTES |
|---|---|---|---|
| 31.9% | 52.6% | 13.8% | 1.7% |

**MIDDLE MANAGEMENT: 39 MINUTES**

| UNDER 10 MINUTES | 10-30 MINUTES | 30-60 MINUTES | OVER 60 MINUTES |
|---|---|---|---|
| 18.1% | 40.8% | 33.8% | 7.3% |

**NON-OFFICIALS: 39 MINUTES**

| UNDER 10 MINUTES | 10-30 MINUTES | 30-60 MINUTES | OVER 60 MINUTES |
|---|---|---|---|
| 15.8% | 41.8% | 34.5% | 7.9% |

## EM Boosts Productivity

Experts predict that capital expenditures for office workers will multiply by 1990.[10] However, organizations using electronic mail can expect to cut their operating costs because EM will increase their overall productivity in a number of ways. Studies show that because up to 90 percent of all business documents are for internal company use, electronic mail reduces the number and costs of office memos and telephone calls by as much as 25 percent. In one organization, personnel send and receive an average of 24 electronic messages each day.[11] Electronic mail significantly reduces the time spent on paperwork in this organization, as well as the use of paper, internal paper correspondence/mail service, and photocopying.

Electronic mail also reduces the amount of filing space necessary in an office, as well as labor costs that result when it is necessary to move an office to another location. Systems with advanced features allow salespeople to preformat and store (electronic) office forms, then bring them up on a monitor to be filled out. Once filled out, the forms can be refiled within the system, and the information accessed by other people and acted upon. EM systems also provide and update directories, eliminating the need to print and reprint such material periodically. Such tangible benefits help justify the equipment costs of EM systems.

Many aspects of electronic mail combine to increase productivity: (1) time saved communicating, (2) instant access to information sources, (3) ability to bridge time zones in reaching personnel who are traveling, and (4) ability to access expertise that is unavailable except via electronic communications. In addition, managers and supervisors using automated messaging systems have a broader span of control. They can track more people and projects, and fewer supervisors are required to manage a given quantity of work. Increased productivity is the result.

Even managers who say that EM is "overrated" find that it increases productivity. One such individual, a Federal Aviation Administration (FAA) administrator whose staff offices are dispersed over a large area, admits that EM has reduced the frequency of demands on him. He now holds two, instead of three, staff meetings each week, and leaves individual or group electronic messages for his staff without writing memos or waiting to call meetings. In addition, EM has saved his staff time in responding to memos and carrying their reports to his office.[12]

New communications and information-handling systems have become nearly as important to business as its products and services.[13] These systems allow management to make decisions based on complete information, the issue at the heart of increased productivity/profitability. Electronic mail also:

- Speeds up the decision-making process because there is faster feedback.
- Decreases management "downtime." Downtime refers to those hours when personnel cannot carry out their work because a system is out of order.
- Decreases meeting/travel time and costs.
- Encourages people to find inventive ways of doing their work.

## EM Increases Job Satisfaction

Introducing electronic mail into an organization often creates more time for individual workers and managers. This translates into increased quality and professionalism in their projects because they are better able to catch errors. Managers can also give people immediate feedback on their work, taking a minute to compliment them when they are on track—without interrupting them.

Electronic mail brought unexpectedly gratifying results to the supervisor of a high-tech Silicon Valley public relations agency. She reported not only an increase in the quality of her work but the following other advantages:[14]

- Ability to copy messages effortlessly and forward them to the head of the agency without interrupting him.
- One-time handling of most documents.
- Support for organizing meetings and distributing reports.
- Ability to send articles and press releases to editors by means of an E-COM connection.

## EM Centralizes Organizational Operations

EM is a way to bring similar operations at different company sites under one authority. The following story illustrates this point.

A high-tech manufacturer had been developing educational materials for employee programs at seven locations across the United States and Canada. Preparation of the necessary slides, manuals, handouts, etc., involved graphic arts assistance at each installation and a considerable amount of supervisory time. By centralizing the operation in one office, employing one artist with secretarial skills and using EM, the company was able to realize very substantial savings. Supervisors at each site used EM facilities to send material to the artist to develop for presentation. The artist and supervisors then discussed—again using EM—the various ways of handling the materials. The artist was able to produce text and graphic materials for presentation by using the following tools and introducing a few personal touches:

- A computer with a color graphic display unit.
- Equipment that produced video slides.
- A graphics plotter.
- An electronic copier.

Once copies of the completed materials were produced, they were transmitted electronically to supervisors at each site for approval, then printed and distributed.

## EM Changes Organizational Structure

The traditional barriers that separate executives from middle and lower management are reduced when advanced electronic methods of communication are introduced. EM contributes to a change in the communications patterns of an organization by encouraging a move in the direction of more decentralized information processing, job sharing, and telecommuting. Oftentimes, communication between upper and lower levels of management is improved significantly as a result. In addition, redistribution of personnel created by electronic mail and current communications systems is causing a change in the configuration of organizational structures (see Figure 1.3).

Maintaining a competitive edge in the research and development of a new product requires teamwork. Electronic mail makes teamwork easy and effective by providing people with a "place" to meet whenever necessary and a way to access common files.

The challenge to management in the future will be social rather than technological. Electronic mail affects the "people side" of office automation, improving communication by making it possible to reach others when necessary. Quick and appropriate feedback results in higher-quality work and boosts the morale of those participating in a project.

## EM Aids Sales

Companies that particularly benefit by incorporating electronic mail into their organizational structure are characterized by the following:[15]

- A large sales force.
- Dispersed offices that handle work on a per-project basis.
- Production of goods that require technical and administrative support.
- High administrative overhead.
- Growth of 15 percent or more each year.

This type of company routinely equips its sales force with portable computers that connect to ordinary telephone lines and enable sales personnel to reach company EM systems and databases. While a salesperson is calling on a client, he or she can access accurate information "on the spot," tapping electronically filed product descriptions, company inventories, information on product delivery times, and costs. The tracking functions of an EM system enable management to monitor sales by keeping accurate records of each salesperson's activity. This procedure is more efficient than holding field-to-office telephone conversations.

## FIGURE 1.3

The effects of communication and information technology on business structures.

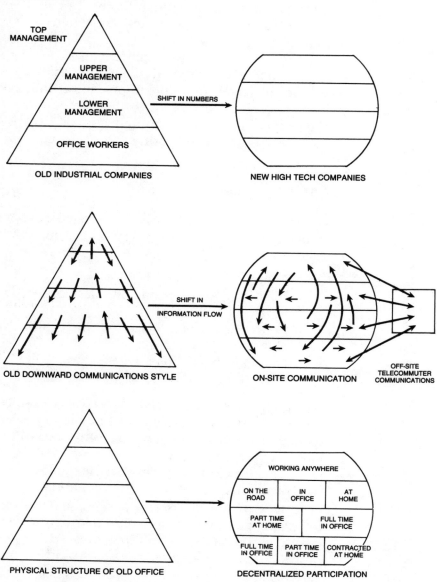

## EM Enhances an Organization's Image

Organizations using advanced technology are perceived as being on the cutting edge in terms of equipment and services. Whether clients are buying pharmaceuticals, bathroom fixtures, or soft drinks, they are usually impressed by salespeople who use a speedy, high-tech messaging system in handling their business.

# HOW EM MEETS SPECIAL NEEDS

### EM Improves the Political Process

Congressmen are using EM systems to improve communications with their constituents. Senator William Sederburg of Michigan, a long-time computer fan, uses an EM software system called Political Forum. He provides his constituents with an electronic bulletin board where he places weekly updates on legislative issues for their reference. "On-line constituents" can also leave confidential messages and requests in Sederburg's electronic mailbox. He uses the same facility to conduct non-scientific polls.[16]

Congressman James Coyne of Pennsylvania keeps terminals in both his Washington and home office locations. By entering Coyne's phone number and password into their terminals, his constituents reach him via the CompuServe™ Information Service of the H&R Block Company. People without computers are allowed to use district library and school computers to reach Coyne's offices. Coyne believes EM has proved particularly important to people with urgent problems, especially those who haven't received an expected monthly social security check.[17]

### EM Links Government Agencies

Many federal government agencies use EM. The Department of Agriculture (USDA) has developed a 3,000-person electronic mailbox system (Comet™) and also uses news-wire database services (ITT Dialcom). Part of this service is searching news articles for words known to be of interest to particular USDA individuals. Articles found to contain the key words are automatically sent to the appropriate mailboxes. The following story demonstrates the usefulness of this service to people under job pressure.

Secretary of Agriculture John R. Block was traveling with his portable computer (Radio Shack Model 100™) in the Midwest on a Sunday evening. When he accessed the USDA electronic messaging facilities for his "mail," Block received news-wire reports that a Chicago meat-packing firm was improperly administering a government food program. With this information in hand, Block was able to send all USDA officials a copy of the original news release and prepare a response for the media by Monday morning.[18]

## EM Improves Communications for the Handicapped

Electronic mail has proved useful to such nonprofit organizations as the Deaf Community Center, a national organization formed to provide aid and training for the deaf.[19] The Center sought a system that would improve its communications with members by providing up-to-date, specialized information and training. By establishing an EM network of 70 terminals in 17 states, the Center was able to offer its members timely information on special programs for the deaf within their own communities and an instructional setting that enabled members to ask questions of an instructor and get answers back rapidly. Among the benefits noted by members were improved reading and writing skills and "feelings of [personal] freedom." Because of the nature of its membership, however, older people required one-on-one training in using the system in their own homes, and the manual needed to be rewritten to match the users' capabilities.

## EM Links Bulletin Board System (BBS) Enthusiasts

An electronic bulletin board system (BBS) is a file that can be established within an electronic mail system, a computer-based messaging system, or a teleconferencing system. Depending on the purpose of the BBS, people log on to place or retrieve information, messages, or other offerings. In addition to being a forum for discussion, a BBS usually provides users with a software library that can be transferred to the person's computer memory storage.

This well-established networking pastime is popular among members of scientific, academic, and other communities, as well as personal computer (PC) owners. It has also found an important niche in business by supplementing other office information systems, and as a way for companies to promote their products and services.

There are numerous commercial BBSs and hundreds of free or minimal-cost public bulletin boards available to the average computer user across the country. Many of these provide private electronic mailboxes for people calling in. CompuServe™ National Bulletin Board and The Source™ Post are two popular commercial BBSs.

When information or messages are placed in the system, the BBS organizes this material and makes it available to others. A BBS can be considered interactive in the sense that users can both place and retrieve information. Though BBS programs differ, the caller is typically permitted to choose a function on a menu, and is then coached by the system. System functions can include: scanning topics, reading or posting messages, replying to messages, or requesting help.

On private BBSs, calls are usually accepted one at a time, often creating accessing problems. Other problems with BBSs are accidental or deliberate computer damage or disk erasure and obscene messages entered by callers.

## EM Changes Stock Market Operations

EM and other telecommunications systems are affecting American Stock Exchange operations and, some say, transforming the stock market itself. The forces of computer technology and the "40-button telephone" are enabling traders "to sweep hundreds of millions of dollars out of one group of stocks and into another in a matter of minutes," according to Desmond Smith, writing for the *New York Times Magazine*.[20] He makes the following points concerning the effect of current messaging technology on stock market operations:

- Communications need no longer be carried out in one room.
- Speed of market operations forces market movement.
- Assets are managed differently. (Institutions have become responsible for more than three-fourths of trading on a given day.)
- Large-scale aggressive trading is causing the line between speculation and investment to blur.
- Individual investors are beginning to manage their personal investments from their living room computers by using totally automated exchange functions. This is creating a fear that Wall Street may become what market analyst Ulrich Weil calls "the great casino in the sky, a gigantic apparatus for legitimized legal gambling on a worldwide scale." (A fourfold increase in the PC market expected by 1988 is certain to accelerate the trend.[21])
- Computers can help the investor manage risk by changing variables and asking, "What if . . . ?" questions.
- Small brokerage houses that are unable or unwilling to invest in "new technology" are being put out of business.
- Discount brokers banking on volume are taking business away from old, established firms.
- Technology is making the over-the-counter (OTC) market for securities a challenge to other stock exchanges.

The private individual with a home computer and modem can obtain reports on more than 3,100 common stocks via The Source™ stock market service.[22] By keying into a particular database through this service, the user can find each week approximately 55 items of updated information about common stocks from the New York, American, and over-the-counter exchanges. These items include data on price, volume, trends, earnings, dividends, and many other areas.

**FIGURE 1.4**

CBX (computerized branch exchange) telecommuting home of the future.

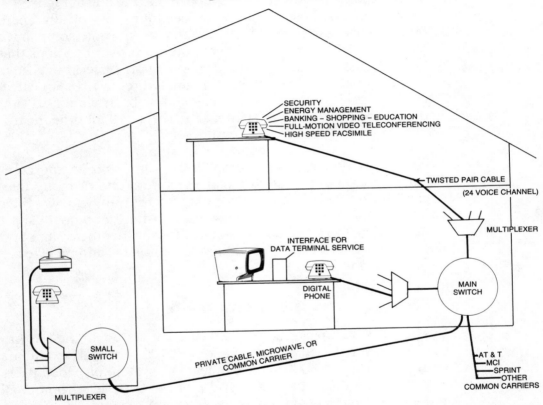

## EM Permits Telecommuting

"Telecommuting" means working at a home or other terminal and interacting with an employer via computer telecommunications. It is one of the more talked-about business practices evolving as EM popularity grows. Proponents claim that telecommuting will eventually transform American working and family patterns both by saving people commuting time and costs and by helping to keep families together. A high estimate pegs the total number of telecommuters in mid-1985 at 100,000. This number is expected to grow to 10 million by 1990.[23] The future telecommuter's home might well be equipped like the one in Figure 1.4.

Companies whose employees telecommute typically claim productivity increases of 20 to 80 percent, and some have claimed increases of 150 percent and more. Organizations that have carried out formal computer homework experiments have generally connected employee terminals directly to their central computers. Productivity was calculated by tracking an employee's keystrokes at a terminal and the length of time the terminal was connected to the computer.

Employees who have stand-alone equipment often work independently, then transfer completed assignments to the company's computer. Legal secretarial work is one of many telecommuting areas becoming popular. Secretaries who own their own equipment and choose to work part-time, or who must remain home to attend to the needs of family members, are good candidates. Law offices send them assignments and receive the completed work via EM.

## EM Organizes the Sporting Life

The 1984 Olympics electronic messaging system in the Los Angeles area reached athletes at some 1,700 terminals extending over an area of 4,000 square miles. The system provided users with both person-to-person and point-to-point electronic mail service, and enabled them to access event schedules and scores and to request other services. It also allowed them to be linked to a radio paging system and telex service.[24]

# 2 Electronic Mail: Past, Present, and Future

## THE DEVELOPMENT OF EM

Although the roots of electronic messaging reach back to the development of telegraphic and facsimile transmission in the mid-1800s, current EM technology and communications networking systems evolved largely after World War II.

Telex and facsimile (fax), commercial messaging systems which predate that time, transmit messages from one place to another (station-to-station) and require senders and recipients to be on-line at the same time. Hence they are often described as being like "sending mail over the telephone." Telex and fax are still widely used, and updated models with sophisticated features found in later EM systems remain adequate for the fast-messaging needs of many organizations.

Electronic mail faced a number of problems during its early years. First, there were design and equipment limitations. Much of the equipment and many networks were not designed to interact, and EM systems were not used to their best advantage. Second, because vendors and consultants lacked technical expertise, they provided limited training to users and little feedback to the industry regarding users' experiences. Third, managers tended to shy away from the computer keyboard, and users generally failed to message effectively.

There have also been psychological, economic, and political obstacles to EM growth. Some governments have attempted to maintain control over internal communications technology and stymie its use, fearing that foreign powers or multinational corporations would communicate directly with their citizens and influence internal politics.

Objection to the introduction of new technology has sometimes come from religious leaders who believe innovation will challenge their traditional values. When telephones were first introduced into Saudi Arabia, for example, conservative religious leaders objected to them as being tools of the devil. But the prince who was charged with the task of running his country's phone system hit upon the idea of reading the Koran—the country's primary religious text—over the telephone. How could anyone object to a device that brought the words of the Koran over long distances to the faithful?

When more-sophisticated EM systems became available in the 1970s, the pioneer users were financially strong organizations that depended on swift, efficient communications. These included airline, transportation, insurance, and publishing companies, as well as the U.S. government.

Some organizations, recognizing the need to upgrade their internal communications systems, piggybacked EM systems onto existing word processing and office automation systems. They found that work took less time, communication improved, and the savings in paper and paperwork, as well as in postal costs, justified their expenditures. Trade magazines and consultants reported on these measurable gains in office productivity and stimulated broader business interest in EM.

During the 1980s, electronic mail gained worldwide acceptance, influencing the international business, scientific, academic, and political communities, as well as affecting global thinking and interaction. Daniel Bell of Harvard University believes that the telecommunications revolution is binding countries closer together in economic interdependence, and that the real challenge is "to maintain economic stability during this difficult transition period, to deal with the very real human problems, and to take advantage of many new marketing opportunities being created by this new revolution."[1]

Will availability of information help people and governments make wiser decisions for the world community? The hope is that electronic mail and teleconferencing networks throughout the world can help unify humankind by building links among peoples that will help them avoid misunderstandings and conflict.

Today, the pressure for fast information exchange, coupled with available and less costly technologies, has made it economically feasible for all sectors of the economy to use EM equipment. Future office systems will also include teleconferencing, voice mail, advanced systems for interrelating files, speaker screens, and graphics transmission equipment.

## EM Becomes User Friendly

The communications/computer jargon that has developed along with computer hardware confounds many people, and discourages those with nontechnical backgrounds from exploring new equipment and systems. Each new generation of computer technology, however, becomes more user friendly. As Professor Bell has noted:

> Technological revolutions always seem to get easier for succeeding generations. One great advantage of this revolution is that it is self-simplifying. New fifth-generation computers, due in the 1990s, will break down most of the communication barriers. You will be able to sit in front of a computer and tell it what you want to do in your natural language. The computer will then interpret and act on your instructions.[2]

Today, organizations hire consultants who are experienced in setting up communications networks to evaluate their EM needs and recommend the appropriate tools and techniques for using them. In large corporations, a consultant may also train personnel in using the system being implemented and establish a company information center. In fact, observers see an information systems management position evolving to answer this overall need.[3]

Electronic mail systems will become increasingly user friendly as equipment features such as screen control aids and "soft keys" are incorporated into more computer systems. Screen aids include display windows, devices for manipulating graphics and color, and icons. Soft keys are function keys whose meaning or function the user can change.

Another user-friendly trend is to make EM systems available in public places such as libraries and hotels. Viewdata-type equipment placed in kiosks in hotel/motel lobbies is expected to enable guests and area residents to access databases, handle their banking needs, and send and receive electronic mail.

## Office Equipment Becomes More Compatible

A serious problem has been the inability of one office device to interact or communicate with others. Until recently, office equipment, even "brother-and-sister" equipment produced by the same manufacturer, was often incompatible.

The problem was that hardware and software, as well as codes and signaling systems designed for devices, were not created with interactivity as the objective. Their design depended instead on a host of marketing and manufacturing considerations. Because of the resulting incompatibility, potential EM users waited on the sidelines to see which equipment would dominate the market, and what the EM experiences of other organizations would be.

C. A. Ross of Honeywell vividly illustrates the importance of compatibility in describing the plight of a national sales manager who was given only one day to prepare a difficult report explaining why his company's sales performance did not conform to the projections of the district managers.[4] Ross contends that the manager could have handled this request with dispatch if his terminal had been compatible with the company's central and regional computer databases.

He first could have determined the demographics of each sales area by using a database service, then checked competitors' annual reports for their performances. He could also have used the projections filed by district managers in the company's databases and checked his staff's monthly results and analyses. Finally, he could have analyzed his figures through spreadsheet calculations and transaction processing. Ross fails to add that the manager might have completed his project even faster by using the word processing facilities of his EM system to write his report, then sending it in electronically as well.

## EM Software Is Becoming More Intelligent

The development of EM systems has been somewhat limited by the difficulty of writing some aspects of software programs. For example, while it is easy to design software that instructs an addressee's printer to turn on, it is far more complex to write software that controls any subsequent printing operations.

The telecommunications industry is producing software programs that allow organizations to establish private databases, and database management systems (DBMSs) that enable users to control access to information. These are growing in popularity, along with spreadsheet software programs and computer-based message systems (CBMSs).

Communication-networking programs meant to be "electronic working environments" for brainstorming, "thought processing," and problem solving are also being developed. One of these, CROSS/POINT™, enables individuals to organize, reorganize, and chart information, data, and ideas in a number of ways. A person can work from any point within the system, retrace steps, add more information, and then reconfigure it. This type of software program encourages analytical thinking and makes available the broadest variety of choices for solving problems. It also helps the user choose the best alternative. Such a communication-networking software system can also be electronically linked with other systems to form a larger network.

Artificial intelligence (AI) systems provide another approach to organizing and evaluating information. These are software programs that can recognize appropriate ideas and respond with data or questions that lead to decision making and problem solving. AI systems have proved useful in robotics. When they are part of "expert systems" (databases with highly specialized information), computers can be questioned on a particular topic. Although artificial intelligence is still in its very early developmental stages, it is expected to be an integral part of general computer operations by the 1990s.

Regional medical computer networks using such communication-networking software programs exist at Duke University

Medical School in North Carolina and Methodist Hospital in Houston. Dr. Patrick J. Hogan, a teacher at the Texas Heart Institute, is developing a decision analysis computer program that will allow patients to participate in the diagnostic process.[5]

The future will see large-scale integration of the electronic components or chips at the heart of computerization, as well as upgraded software that will enable users to maximize the potential within current hardware configurations.[6]

## Transmission Is Becoming Standardized

In the past, a serious limitation of EM systems was that they operated at a rate of 300 baud (transmission speed in bits per second), making the communications process quite slow by today's standards. As a result, equipment was tied up for long periods, and users' monthly telephone bills were high. Today, typical transmission rates range from 1,200 to 9,600 baud, enabling users to send vast amounts of data almost instantaneously. In addition, devices have been developed that both link equipment to network lines and cut transmission time and storage costs by holding messages until night hours when those costs are lowest. As a result, it is currently possible to send a 10-page report across the country via EM for a fraction of overnight express service charges.

By the early 1980s, manufacturers realized that it was to their benefit to produce communicating devices designed to interface with similar equipment, international networks, and international postal organizations. Thus, industry leaders encouraged international standards organizations to create technical design standards that would create a global networking system (see Table 2.1). At the same time, manufacturers began to create hardware and software that bridged gaps in the telecommunications process.

Among the standards that have been developed, the X.400 Message Handling Facility (MHF) has received the broadest endorsement. It was developed and approved in October 1984 by the Consultative Committee for International Telephony and Telegraphy (CCITT) of the International Telecommunications Union (ITU) in Geneva, Switzerland. The X.400 is widely sup-

**TABLE 2.1. National and International Standards Organizations**

NBS — United States National Bureau of Standards
Government agency that sets standards for equipment the federal government purchases; these standards do not apply to the Defense Department

ISO — International Standards Organization
Voluntary international organization with committees in participating countries

CCITT — Consultative Committee for International Telephony and Telegraphy
Part of the United Nations International Telecommunications Union (ITU); membership includes national representatives and private company, scientific, and trade association representatives

ANSI — American National Standards Institute
Voluntary organization of manufacturers, communications networks, and users

IEEE — Institute of Electrical and Electronic Engineers (International)
Professional society of individuals that issues its own standards and contributes to ANSI

EIA — Electronic Industries Association (United States)
U.S. manufacturers' trade association; also a contributor to ANSI

ECMA — European Computer Manufacturers Association
Small group of primarily European computer suppliers

EMA — Electronic Mail Association
Association organized to promote electronic mail, including standards

ported by major companies such as AT&T, GTE, and ITT; timesharing services like CompuServe and Tymshare's OnTyme℠ ; and the postal, telephone, and telegraph services of many countries.

Once the X.400 is implemented, specialists believe that it will create outstanding opportunities for using electronic mail systems internationally. It is expected to make it possible for various communications networks to interconnect and provide a universal system. Within such a system, people using incompatible computer-based messaging systems (CBMSs) and both current and older electronic messaging systems will be able to exchange information files, voice, text, and graphics. The X.400 is also expected to upgrade older facsimile and telex communications systems. Recipients will be addressed by name and other ID rather than by terminal or station alone. It will also be possible to encode messages placed on the system (see Figure 2.1).

**FIGURE 2.1**

X.400 Message Handling Facility as a global system.

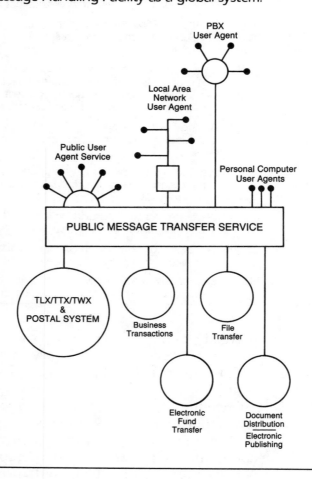

When implemented throughout the industry, the X.400 standard will:

- Provide intermediate transfer agents that handle and relay messages from points of origin to destinations.
- Relay procedures between networks.
- Verify procedures for electronic mailbox addresses.

- Establish codes for communicating between systems, as well as for converting digital signals to voice messages.
- Standardize options, such as grade of service, security priorities, multidestination delivery, and cross-referencing.

The integrated services digital network (ISDN) is another approach to standardization that is being developed by AT&T and most other major telecommunications companies. Because it is intended to manage the integrated digital technology that handles voice, data, music, and video transmissions, it is expected to deliver a number of advanced customized telecommunications services to business, government agencies, banks, and news services as well as to residential customers. Many companies believe this technology possesses all the ingredients necessary for total end-to-end information processing and will serve the bulk of business communications needs by carrying the high-speed transmission of large amounts of data from computer to computer.

Key to ISDN development will be new telephone central office (CO) switching equipment and digital equipment, coupled with a special signaling system that connects a central telephone office to homes and businesses.

One early system, called DOV (data over voice), is an ISDN service providing a two-way channel on any telephone/cable TV line. It can serve many people at one time and allows simultaneous use of a telephone line for information distribution and telephone calls.

# NEW EM TRANSMISSION TECHNOLOGY ————

Lightweight personal communications devices such as cellular telephones are now being used to transmit electronic mail. Cellular telephones enable individuals in moving vehicles to access and interact with EM networks anywhere in the world. Previously, one powerful transmitter reached car telephones within a large geographical area. The cellular telephone system divides that area into smaller zones and uses lower-powered transmitters to cover each zone. Because the same frequencies are available in each zone, there is no signal interference. Cellular telephones require considerably less power to operate than traditional car radio systems, and a significantly higher number of people can access a cellular radio system at the same time. Voice transmission is also of a higher quality in these systems. Thus, cellular telephone systems are expected to become increasingly popular for both home use and in business.

The personal, mobile satellite telephone is a new "instantaneous communication device" on the horizon. Using a mobile satellite telephone, a person will be able to stand anywhere in the world and beam a message up to a satellite. The satellite will relay the message to a remotely located telephone utility that will complete the call. A satellite telephone will thus allow the user to reach an EM network anywhere in the world.

Another technology expected to affect electronic mail is a facsimile device that accepts radio signals. This equipment will effectively eliminate the need for telephones or cables and will produce hard copy that can be filed for future reference. These facsimile devices have been used experimentally in police cars to receive all-points bulletins and photos of wanted persons.

Cable TV (CATV) is being used in a number of cities to interconnect high-speed data transmission systems on a point-to-point/point-to-multipoint basis. The largest such system is available in New York City, where users bypass local telephone networks when they transmit their electronic mail. Transmission costs are low because users are charged by the thousands of bits of data transmitted per second and transmission is almost instantaneous.

Most of the U.S. CATV systems in current use provide broadcast (one-way) service primarily to deliver entertainment programs. Newer, more-sophisticated, interactive (two-way) CATV systems are now available for communicating. They provide subscribers with videotext systems that offer shop-at-home, bank-at-home, information retrieval, and other services. Videotext is a service that uses part or all of a television screen for information displays. (See Figure 2.2 for evolving telecommunications trends.)

## FIGURE 2.2
Evolving telecommunications trends.

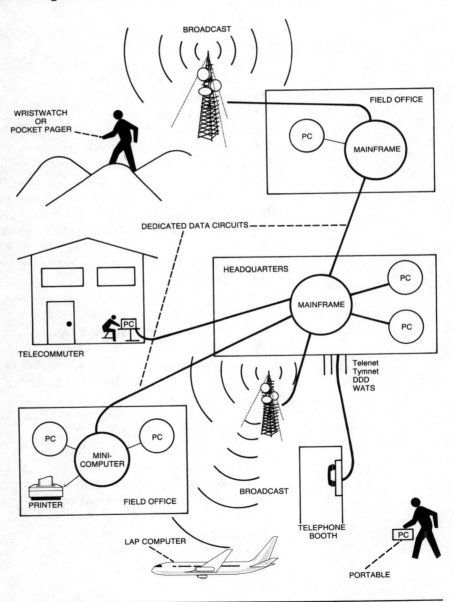

## FUTURE TRENDS

Consensus is that electronic mail/messaging will continue to mushroom as:

- The telecommunications industry standardizes its hardware.
- Manufacturers upgrade EM-related technology using PBXs and facsimile equipment.
- Technology advances—particularly those developments related to silicon chips.
- Integrated communications is facilitated by the use of photons (light) rather than electrons as the transmission medium within computer circuitry. Circuitry that handles photons will eliminate the shortcomings of metal wiring and allow increased amounts of data to be transmitted at higher rates. Light is currently used for transmitting data within fiber optic long-haul and local area networks.[7]
- Large-scale integration (LSI) devices used in electronic circuitry decrease in cost.
- Personal computer (PC) use increases in popularity.
- Local area networks (LANs), computer-based message systems, and intelligent copiers become better known in business and gain in popularity.
- Business competition increases, forcing organizations to keep in step with demands for faster access to and retrieval of information.
- Office automation becomes the norm rather than the exception.
- Office costs continue to rise, and white-collar management is pressured to achieve greater productivity.
- The trend toward geographical dispersion of organizations continues, even as some organizational operations are centralized and others decentralized.
- It is recognized that distributed processing systems are the optimum computer network arrangement for the corporate environment.

- Development of software programs continues to make it easier for untrained people to use computers.
- The advantages and applications of electronic mail become better known.

# PART TWO

# Electronic Mail Operations

What are the components of an electronic mail system? How does electronic mail work? What systems and services provide electronic mail? How do messages travel? What are the different types of electronic networks? What are electronic meetings?

# 3 Electronic Mail: The Communications Link of the Automated Office

The largest group of electronic mail users are currently found in the automated offices of the business world. This part of the book examines the various office systems, transmission equipment, and networking and communications techniques that businesses use in electronic messaging. The same or similar systems and methods are used by people in government, universities, organizations, hobby clubs, etc.

Office automation (OA) is "modern electronic business and communications equipment coupled with appropriate procedures which provide significantly improved office productivity," according to Charles H. Divine, Director, Exploratory Development, American Telecom.[1] Electronic mail serves the "people side" of office automation by letting people communicate whenever they need to and from wherever they are located.

Office automation systems are often classified by the types of businesses they serve and the way in which they handle communications. The following are three common system designations:

- Dedicated office automation systems – in-house systems dedicated to carrying out specific functions. They have become an economic necessity to small businesses, and a means for reducing the staffs of very large organizations.
- Office automation/data processing (OA/DP) systems – basic data processing systems onto which OA systems have been grafted. OA/DPs are usually found in medium to large business organizations.

- OA/PBX systems – systems generally built upon internal computerized telephone networks.

## COMPONENTS OF AN ELECTRONIC MAIL SYSTEM

The following individual component systems make up the larger automated office configuration:

- Word processing
- Data processing
- Records processing
- Printing
- Scanning/sending (e.g., facsimile)
- Administrative support
- Decision support
- Voice mail
- Teleconferencing

(The equipment that manages these systems is discussed in Chapter 4.)

**Word Processing.** A word processing system provides document formatting procedures and allows a user to produce complicated multipage documents. Editing is swift and simple, and specialized software programs are available that check for correct spelling.

**Data Processing.** A data processing system controls and stores a great quantity of information. A multitude of specialized software application programs are available for different professions, e.g., business, medicine, dentistry, and banking. Data processing terminals are among the most common OA workstations. Their "soft" keys can be assigned and reassigned specialized functions and they provide users with time-saving operational shortcuts.

**Records Processing.** Records processing means establishing records, rearranging the information within them, and interrelating the files of various organizational departments. To store information off-line, some organizations use computer output microfilm (COM) units to create back-up copies of information. COMs reduce and record directly onto film the vast amounts of material produced by a computer, significantly reducing storage needs.

**Printing.** Printers used in automated offices vary widely. Daisy wheel and dot matrix printers are popular impact printers. More costly laser and ink-jet printers are usually shared by many users in automated offices. Their speed, quietness, quality of printing, paper handling capabilities, and varieties of font types make them especially suited to high-volume production. Some versatile laser and jet printers are replacing offset printing for certain applications.

**Scanning.** Scanning systems pick up images and convert them to signals for transmission to compatible terminals that produce copies.

**Administrative Support.** Administrative support capabilities vary widely in automated office systems. Popular features permit users to:

- Schedule activities for groups of people.
- Provide sign-in and sign-out sheets.
- Carry daily updating on the status of projects.
- Keep tickler files.
- Set up meetings by comparing different people's schedules.

**Decision Support.** Decision support systems include functions that aid in group decision making, such as polling. They also include specific functions that let users:

- Carry out mathematical calculations and integrate them into other textual or graphics materials.
- Design, structure, and display spreadsheets.
- Produce graphics and project schedules.

**Voice Mail (VM).** VM systems, described in detail in Chapter 4, can be part of a company's telephone service. Most systems currently available cannot file messages in EM document files or add comments to stored messages and forward them to other individuals. It is likely that future generations of voice mail equipment will offer these services, however.

**Teleconferencing.** Computer teleconferencing systems enable participants to "meet" on-line via their computer terminals. Audio teleconferencing is a means for several people to meet over the telephone. Video teleconferencing transmits both images and voices as part of an electronic meeting.

The equipment that delivers OA systems is evaluated both by its features and by the way it interacts with other office devices.

## AUTOMATED OFFICE CONFIGURATIONS

Two basic equipment configurations have evolved for automated offices. The first is a centralized or host-controlled arrangement that is usually referred to as a management information system (MIS). The equipment in a centralized system is connected to and controlled by a main computer—usually a mainframe or minicomputer that is responsible for setting up communications links, storing software, running disk drives, and managing printers and other peripheral devices. The terminals in this type of arrangement are called "dumb" terminals because they have no processing capability (intelligence) of their own, but rely entirely on the host processor to carry out their instructions (see Figure 3.1).

The management information system has been favored by the data processing staffs that program computers and control information flow in corporations. There are distinct technical advantages to having a central host system support electronic mail features, although there is one serious disadvantage. When the main processor is down, the equipment associated with it becomes inoperative. Another drawback to a centralized system is that an operator must often be conversant with a complex computer language in order to interact with a mainframe.

**FIGURE 3.1**

A management information system (MIS).

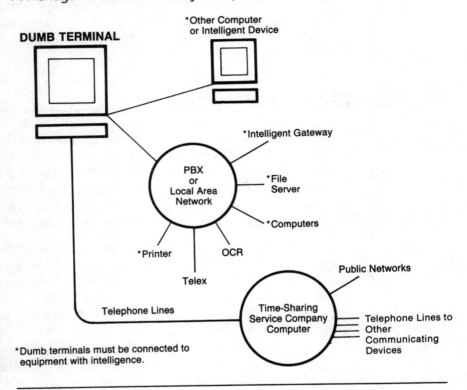

The second system arrangement is known as a "shared resource" or a "distributed processing" network. Each computer or intelligent device in this type of configuration has its own program capabilities and is managed with simple languages.

A shared resource network relies on the host computer only when users need to retrieve documents and graphics that have been filed away in the system memory, or when they need to use the network to access a database.

If one device or unit within a shared resource network is down, other devices continue to operate. Office managers tend to prefer the shared resource approach to the MIS approach because it is more reliable and because it approximates the traditional work arrangement, in which tasks are parceled out for workers to return completed to a supervisor. The growing popularity and usefulness of PCs in automated offices makes the case for a shared resource network even stronger. (See Figure 3.2 for a diagram of terminal-to-terminal EM within central and distributed processing systems.)

## AUTOMATED WORKSTATIONS

Workstations define the automated office. What is the most functional workstation? It depends on the tasks that need to be performed and the people who do them. There is a theory in the communications industry, popular with computer manufacturer NBI, that there are three major groups of office workers requiring special types of workstations. They are:

- Secretaries and clerical workers who need word processing equipment for volume production, and who must be able to circulate their work when it is completed.
- Executives and managers who must analyze numbers, prepare reports, and share information.
- Knowledge or key workers, such as engineers and technicians, who must integrate many different kinds of information and who require a number of "windows" on their monitors (see Figure 3.3) for reference purposes.

All three categories benefit from the ease of communication that electronic mail provides.

## WHAT USERS LOOK FOR

First and foremost, users look for reliability when they are choosing office automation equipment. Price considerations, appropriate functions, and ease of use follow in importance.[2]

## FIGURE 3.2

Terminal-to-terminal electronic mail within central and distributed processing.

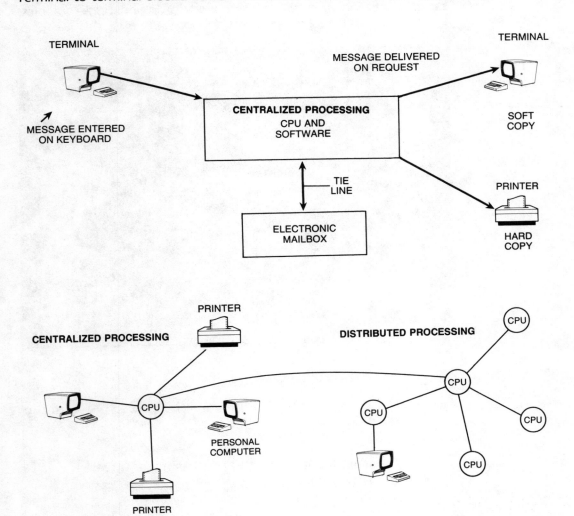

**FIGURE 3.3**

Separate "windows" on the NBI System One monitor enable simultaneous viewing of many different kinds of information—graphics, spreadsheet calculations, document development, etc.

Users also agree that OA systems must be able to perform the following functions:

- Word processing
- Database management and processing
- Administrative support
- Financial analysis
- Decision support
- Electronic mail and computer teleconferencing, as well as the ability to operate remotely located equipment via telecommunications

# EM ARCHITECTURE AND COMPONENTS ─────

Electronic mail "architecture" is the structural design of an EM system. The following elements are essential to the architecture of advanced EM systems:

- Hardware – the machinery in a system that permits information storage and transmission.
- Hardware interfaces – the plugs and cables that connect equipment components. These are important because the equipment interface of one configuration, having a particular size, shape, and number of wires, will work only with devices that have the same characteristics or standard. The RS-232C standard cable connector and the increasingly common RJ11S telephone jack are among the more widely used interconnecting devices.
- Software – programs of instructions that control and guide computer operations.
- Software interface – a program that controls the way a computer interacts with other programs it uses.
- Communications interface – converts signals generated by a keyboard (bits and control signals) into pulses that a network will accept.
- Communications protocol – the signaling procedure that enables computers and terminals to talk to one another. A protocol converter interprets this procedure so that computers using unlike signals can communicate with each other.
- Coding – As each letter or number is typed on a keyboard, it is coded. The coding identifies the sender, recipient, and a host of other information that is transmitted across the system architecture. Older messaging systems require a user to enter the complete routing coding each time a message is sent.
- Data code – a binary representation of a letter or number that is used by a particular computer and the devices associated with it. ASCII (pronounced "askey")

and EBCDIC (pronounced "ebseedick") are widely used data codes.

- Machine language – defines the instructions that a computer can carry out. The multitude of machine languages has created communications incompatibility problems among computers. This shortcoming can be bridged by emulators, however. An emulator is circuitry that mimics the machine language of one computer so that a second computer can talk to it.
- Operating system – enables a computer to understand the operating instructions it receives.
- Programming language – used to develop programs for computers. Language incompatibility arises when hardware and software companies develop their own language programming "dialects." The answer to this problem lies in the adoption of common computer language standards.
- Storage media standard – refers to the design of disks and tapes used to store computer memory. Unfortunately, once these media have data recorded on them, they will generally work well only with the equipment used in recording. Half-inch magnetic tape used on some mini and mainframe computers is an exception, however, and can be used with various types of equipment.

## HOW ONE USES EM

All EM systems require users to follow specific "log-on" or connect procedures before receiving or creating messages. Users log onto or access a system by presenting a name or identification code, or both. For security purposes, some systems require several passwords.

Before creating a message, it is necessary to enter the addressee's name or coded address. Once the system has verified the address and authorization, it will permit the sender to create and transmit a message. The system then holds that mail until the recipient requests that it be displayed on the monitor, printed out, or preserved in an electronic file.

Typical commands used in sending electronic mail include the following:

- Display Directory – shows the name, system address, company status (sometimes), location, and telephone number of everyone on the system.
- Preview – displays the total number of messages waiting to be read or sent, the names of message originators, and mail that is marked "urgent."
- Compose – prompts the writer for all parts of a message (e.g., address, text, priority, group code, security level, etc.).
- Display – shows a list of file documents and a distribution list or directory.
- Send Message – puts the message in an addressee's electronic mailbox and offers the sender such options as: indication of message priority, courtesy or blind copies, automatic receipt when a message has been read, or "request reply."
- Forward Message – allows a message to be read by one person and then passed along to others.
- Help – brings on-line instructions and options onto the monitor.
- Edit – allows a writer to modify text and message address.
- Timed Message Delivery – specifies the hour a message should be sent.
- Group – allows message "broadcasting" to a specific group of people.
- Note – alerts the recipient of a schedule, etc.
- Copy – sends copies to designated names.
- Registered/Forced Reply – informs a sender when a message has been received, and in some cases requires the recipient to reply.
- Scan – displays message headings or summaries of messages on file, permitting an individual to check them by sender, date, subject, or text.

- Retrieve – prompts a writer for search criteria and searches one or more files.
- File – stores messages in files and creates new ones when necessary.
- Classification – provides priority designation such as confidential, nonconfidential, and personal.
- Quit – stops an operation and allows the operator to leave the EM system.

When the user receives or reads electronic mail, the following options are usually available:

- Accepted/Received – notifies sender that a message has been received. It may allow the recipient such options as: replying, forwarding, filing, leaving a message in the mailbox, or deleting messages.
- Again – allows the second reading of a message.
- Answer – helps compose a reply.
- Print – tells the computer or other equipment to print a copy of a specific message.
- Hold – indicates that a message has been read, and the recipient is waiting to reply.
- Withdraw – retracts one or more previously sent messages from EM boxes when addressees have not acknowledged receiving them.
- Append/Attach – allows a note to be added at the bottom of a completed message, and the total message forwarded.
- Forward – routes a message to other designated people.

# SOFTWARE FACILITIES PROVIDED BY AN EM SYSTEM

Early EM equipment (teletypewriters and facsimile devices) provides one-to-one communication and, as in a telephone call, requires users to be on-line simultaneously. The advantage of this real-time link, known as synchronous communication, is that a channel remains open and available for both parties to use. This is well suited for communicating during crises, for teaching, and in some conferencing situations. Real-time communicating forces people to schedule their sessions when time is available for both parties, however, and can create inconvenience.

In contrast with real-time communication, store-and-forward capability allows messages to wait in an addressee's electronic mailbox until they are requested. They are then brought up on a monitor, delivered by phone, or printed—depending on the equipment being used and the commands it accepts. Messages that appear on a monitor or in audio format are known as "soft copy." Printed messages or information is called "hard copy."

Store-and-forward messaging instructions can be written into a computer software program or provided by a personal computer that operates with automatic dialing-and-answering devices or by a computer network service. Network services are considered to be good store-and-forward points because their switching equipment can modify incoming signals. In this way dissimilar receiving terminals can accept them. This is called protocol conversion.

To deliver an incoming message, the network computer searches its directory for the receiving terminal's technical characteristics or "asks" the receiving terminal for this information before delivering a message. Networks that distribute hard-copy advertising or informational material for clients have addressee lists on file. In some instances recipients dial in for information and messages.

The following software systems are among the many that provide various types of EM:

Profs™ – IBM
InfoMail™ – Bolt, Baranek, and Newman
Comet™ – Computer Corporation of America
Cybergam™ – Cybertex Computer Products
EMS™ – Datapoint Corporation
Fox™ – Computer Projects, Inc.
Microcourier™ – Microcom, Inc.
Messenger™ – Nestar Systems
Omnicom™ – On-Line Software International

Integrated Software™ – Prime Computer, Inc.
Mailway™ – Wang Laboratories, Inc.
Inmail™ – Interactive Systems Corporation
Elf™ – Systar Corp.
Mailbox™ – STSC, Inc.
OFIS Information System™ – Burroughs
CEO™ (Comprehensive Electronic Office) – Data General
HPMAIL™ – Hewlett-Packard
DECMail™ – Digital Equipment Corporation

## HARDWARE COMPONENTS OF ADVANCED EM SYSTEMS

The standard computer terminal is made up of a keyboard, monitor (display screen), and printer. Operating as a unit, the three components provide the means for sending and receiving electronic mail. Incoming and outgoing messages are handled by a computer processor that can be located in any one of several places. When a computer processor is located within the terminal unit, it is called an "intelligent" terminal. When processing is carried out in a connected device such as a printer or file server, the terminal is called "dumb."

Both intelligent and dumb terminals can be used to communicate. The Scanset XL™ terminal distributed by Tymshare is an example of a dumb terminal that has been built as a communicating device. It combines terminal and telephone functions, and can be used to send and receive EM and access databases. The Scanset XL™ can also be linked to an intelligent business computer.

**Monitors.** Terminal monitors are sometimes called display screens, video display units (VDUs), or cathode ray tubes (CRTs). They display the text being composed at a terminal keyboard or received in messaging. Once messages are viewed, they can be edited, stored (filed) electronically, forwarded to others as mail, or printed—depending on an operator's instructions.

Monitors are available that display either single lines of text, groups of lines, a page of text, or text and graphics combined. The quality of the images seen on computer monitors is a function of the number of lines on the screen. Since monitors used for computers have many more lines than most TV screens, they provide a viewer with clearer text and pictures, and less flicker. The cost of a monitor varies according to the quality of the cathode ray tube installed or the display technology, as well as the sophistication of the electronics used to support it. Many monitors permit adjustment of letter size, brightness, and letter-background contrast.

**Keyboards.** Computer keyboard layouts vary according to the hardware/software relationships in a system. When keyboard manufacturers promote the "ergonomic" philosophy behind their products, they are referring to design features such as keyboard slope and key size or shape that they believe will make their product comfortable to use.

**Printers.** There are three basic impact printing systems. One system uses a golf ball–like head with rows of letters, numbers, and other characters on its surface. As the ball spins, it strikes a carbon ribbon against paper to print the characters. A second type of impact printer, known as a "daisy wheel," has characters located on the ends of "petals" radiating from a wheel. As the wheel spins, a hammer presses the appropriate petal against a ribbon and onto paper. A third type of impact printing device is known as a matrix printer. Dot matrix printers strike the paper with different combinations of metal pins that create dots in patterns approximating the shape of letters, numbers, and symbols.

Among the nonimpact printers available, there are laser or electronic printers that operate like photocopiers, some using plain paper, others using treated or coated papers. There are also ink-jet printers that spray electronically charged drops of ink through a variable magnetic field. The field controls the shape of the characters.

Lasers and ink-jet printers are expected to show the greatest technological development in coming years because they represent the leading edge in printing technology, include advances in electronic circuitry, and have fewer moving parts.

In electrosensitive printing, dots are charged onto a coated paper, removing part of the coating and leaving a black image. Thermal printing is produced by dots that are burned into a coated paper, causing it to turn black or blue when heat is applied to it. Each of these methods requires specially treated paper.

Considerations in choosing a printer should include the following:

- Determining whether terminals and printers work together.
- Printing quality. Requirements for all types of printing tasks should be kept in mind.
- Speed. This will depend on the need for fast and/or volume production, and the quality desired.
- Supplies. Some printers accept plain bond paper, others require specially treated, more expensive paper.

**Electronic Copier-Printers/Electronic Mail Stations.** In addition to providing fast, quiet, and superior-quality printing, electronic copier-printers can be equipped to act as EM stations in automated offices. Simple units are connected to word and data processors or computers and can only print messages received from them. More complex units perform numerous other functions as well as handling communications.

When used as EM centers, sophisticated copier-printers receive mail, store it in a buffer memory, and send it to the appropriate mailboxes where it is held until recipients request it. Copier-printers typically handle:

- Digital data received from word and data processors.
- Textual material received from optical character recognition (OCR) systems (explained in Chapter 4).
- Information from recorded magnetic media.
- Video raster – coded signaling that produces images (like newspaper pictures) composed of thousands of dots.

Banks and other organizations that require high-volume, high-speed printing for internal messaging/distribution benefit from using copier-printers. The IBM 6670™, Xerox 5700™, and AM International's Document Communications System™ are among popular copier-printer models.

**Computer Disks.** Most computers and word processors store data on "floppy" (soft) or hard disks that resemble small phonograph records. When this data is needed, it is copied onto the terminal microprocessor for use. Once it has been processed, the final text is returned to the disk for storage and future recall. Data remains on the memory disk until the user erases it.

Floppies are formed of a flexible plastic that is coated with magnetic material. Information is recorded on the surface in concentric rings called tracks while the disk is spun at about 300 revolutions per minute (rpm). A "read-write head" records that information while passing above the disk surface (not touching it), and moving in and out on a radial axis. Disks can be erased or re-recorded.

Hard disks spin much faster than soft disks and hold many times the amount of information. Their storage capacity depends on the number of tracks they carry and the density with which information can be recorded on them. Many personal computers that are built to use floppy disks can be upgraded to operate with hard disks. To do this, software and a special module are added.

Optical storage disks, also known as video or laser disks, are a more recent development. They can store encyclopedic amounts of information and make it instantly available through a sophisticated indexing system. It is said that one video disk could store the information in all U.S. telephone books. Some video disks are permanently recorded, others can be re-recorded. Movies and stereo sound are currently the most common optical storage disk applications.

Another storage device is called "bubble memory." Combining semiconductor and magnetic recording techniques, bubble memory systems store bits of information in bubbles that are made to spin in circles past a stationary read-write head. Although comparatively expensive, this type of device allows information stored in the bubble to be retained when power is turned off. Conventional computers must store their information on disks or tapes, or it vanishes when the computer is turned off.

**Modems.** The word "modem" stands for *modulator-demodulator*. A modem is a device that connects computers to telephones or telephone jacks and converts the computer's digital signals to audio tones which the connecting network can accept and transmit. A modem at the receiving end of a transmission converts the audio signals back to digital pulses which the receiving computer can process. Some computers have built-in modems; others require a "plug-in" modem. A plug-in modem is a printed circuit board that is plugged into the back of a computer.

"Intelligent" modems function as a base for an electronic mail system. They can:[3]

- Automatically send and receive EM.
- Store and manage files.
- Generate signals that indicate they are receiving messages.
- Detect errors in messaging.
- Self-test their own operations.

**Multiplexers.** A multiplexer (MUX) is a device designed to increase the capacity of a communications network by allowing many messages to be carried on one line at the same time. The MUX does this by sampling incoming signals, then regrouping and transmitting them as a composite signal. On the receiving end of a transmission, another multiplexer unscrambles the composite signal, reconstructs the messages, and forwards them to addressees.

This process increases a network's efficiency severalfold and is particularly appropriate for use on data-grade telephone lines. By increasing network line capacity, phone companies are able to offer reduced transmission rates. In an automated office setting, multiplexers are placed between a computer's central processing unit and peripheral devices.

Time division multiplexing (TDM) is used on digital networks where each of the several outgoing messages is sampled and assigned a time slot. This allows several slow-speed transmissions to be woven into one high-speed flow (see Figure 3.4). The receiving device knows the duration of each slot and uses this information to reconstruct the messages.

Analog networks, such as traditional telephone lines, use frequency division multiplexing (FDM). In this case, messages that

**FIGURE 3.4**
In time division multiplexing (TDM), messages from each device are allotted a small time interval.

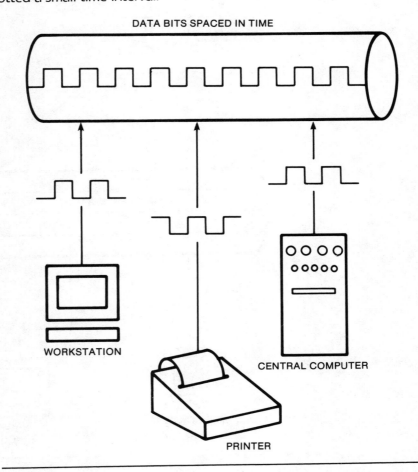

DATA BITS SPACED IN TIME

WORKSTATION

CENTRAL COMPUTER

PRINTER

are assigned different frequencies travel simultaneously over one channel. Each message segment that is multiplexed for transmission is addressed and numbered, and the last segment is identified (see Figure 3.5).

**FIGURE 3.5**

Frequency division multiplexing (FDM) creates small, independent channels by assigning specific frequency bands to the different devices.

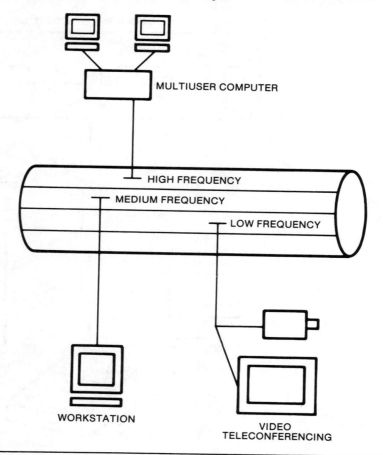

**Computer Processing Unit.** At the heart of an electronic mail system is the central processing unit (CPU), which determines the communications capabilities of a system. Besides controlling the flow of electronic data, the CPU's primary functions include:

- Interfacing with the host computer or peripheral equipment, e.g., terminals, modems, and printers.

- Message switching, or routing of data towards its destination.
- Error control – a systematic way of ensuring that no information is lost during processing.
- Line control – handling computer instructions.
- Assembling characters and messages.
- Data and protocol conversion – procedures that allow communication between equipment that uses different codes.
- Multiplexing signals – sampling and arranging the flow of signals.

When the CPU is part of a "centralized system," it is usually located in a mainframe or minicomputer. A mainframe computer has the benefit of vast memory storage and the power to manage a system of terminals. When a CPU is part of a "distributed network," EM processing power may be found in any intelligent equipment, including microcomputers, word processors, file servers, and electronic printers.

**Communicating Devices.** A number of single-purpose communication devices transmit and receive various kinds of electronic mail. These include:

- Communicating word processors
- Personal and other computers
- Optical character recognition (OCR) systems
- Electronic copiers
- Telephones
- Teletypewriters (teleprinters)
- Facsimile equipment
- Upgraded electronic typewriters

# 4 Electronic Mail Systems and Alternative Services

## EM VIA COMMUNICATING WORD PROCESSORS (CWPs)

Word processors are specialized computer systems built to create, edit, store, and retrieve documents. When they are equipped with specialized software, communicating equipment, cable, and a telephone line for external communication, they are called communicating word processors (CWPs). Eventually, all word processors manufactured are expected to have built-in communications capabilities.

During the last half of the 1970s, business managers connected CWPs so that employees could pass files, documents, and messages among themselves. Most corporations have graduated from word processing operations to more extensive automated operations (see Table 4.1).

CWPs can interact with most other intelligent devices on conventional network systems and can transmit data over microwave links and via satellite (see Figure 4.1). When they are used within a local area network (LAN), CWPs can reach through the network gateway and broadcast messages to many organizations at the same time. Electronic mail software programs for CWPs offer many sophisticated features such as allowing users to:

- Manage memo functions.
- Peruse mail by subject, sender, and date.
- Transmit "envelopes" of files and documents within systems.
- Handle administrative time-management functions such as personal calendaring and room scheduling.

**TABLE 4.1. Electronic Mail Equipment and Processes**

ELECTRONIC MAIL SUMMARY CHART

| DEVICE/PROGRAM | PURPOSE | TYPE OF EM | ENTRY | TRANSMISSION MEDIUM | RECEIVING DEVICE | FORM DELIVERED | EXAMPLE* |
|---|---|---|---|---|---|---|---|
| Dumb terminal | To access EM | Person-to-person | Keyed in at terminal | Public networks, LAN, PBX, DDD, IRC | PC, CBMS, CWP | Soft or hard copy | Silent 700, Radio Shack, Videotext |
| Fully automated office system | To support administration | Person-to-person | Keyed in at terminal | LAN, PBX | Compatible communicating equipment | Soft or hard copy | Datapoint ARC |
| PC-based EM software | To enhance PC operations | Person-to-person | Keyed in at terminal, touch screen, graphics terminal | As above | Terminals, electronic copiers | Soft or hard copy | MIST, Mighty Mail |
| Communicating word processor (CWP) | To transfer files or documents | Station-to-station | Keyed in at CWP | Public networks, LAN, PBX, microwave, satellite | Word processor or other terminal, printer, OCR | Soft or hard copy | Wang Mailway |
| Computer-based message system (CBMS) | To offer premium EM service | Person-to-person | Keyed in at terminal | Utilities, public networks, LAN | Compatible terminals, OCR, teleprinters | Soft or hard copy (as requested) | Dialcom, OnTyme II, Telemail |
| Voice mail/telephone input | To provide independent system | Person-to-person | Voice | Telephone lines | Telephone | Voice | VMX |
| Facsimile (fax) | To provide graphics documentation | Station-to-station | Hard copy | Telephone lines | Compatible machine | Hard copy | Rapicom |
| Teletypewriter (telex) | Independent system | Person or station | Keyed in | IRC, telex, WU | Compatible teleprinter | Hard copy | ASR 33 |
| Optical character recognition (OCR) system | To provide any typed input | Station-to-station | Visual scanning | Direct connection | WP/DP | Electronic form, hard copy | DEST |
| Service | To provide EM to people without computers | Station-hand delivery | Specialized communications equipment | Telex or telephone lines to communications switching center | Depends on service | Hand delivery | ZapMail, MCI Mail, WU Mailgram |

*All examples given, except Videotext and ASR 33, are proprietary products or services.

**FIGURE 4.1**

Automated office environment where communicating devices interact.

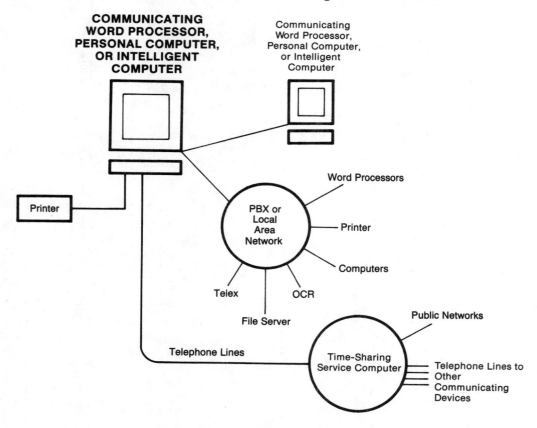

When special software programs are used, communicating word processors and personal computers can also act as full- or part-time hosts for an unattended electronic mail network. Such software programs order the host to turn on its modem and telephone at a given time, establish connections with other units in the system, and poll them for messages. The host also delivers messages to the appropriate machines. Thus, when a system is used for electronic mail after working hours, the users return to work the next morning to find their messages have been delivered and new ones are waiting for them.

# EM VIA COMPUTER-BASED MESSAGING SYSTEMS (CBMSs)

Computer-based message systems (CBMSs) were developed along with communicating word processors during the late 1970s. A CBMS is a sophisticated EM system that incorporates word processing and information-handling operations such as systematic filing and retrieval of information. It can involve such equipment as computers, word processors, OCRs, printers, file servers, telex, and an intelligent gateway (see Figure 4.2). The CBMS has been described as a complete electronic communications working area. As for its acceptance by office workers, one article reported that a CBMS is "taken for granted after 20 hours' use" and that "people are hooked after 50 hours."[1]

By linking equipment with the appropriate hardware and applying effective software programming, it is possible to establish a CBMS by upgrading a communicating word processor system. However, it is sometimes better for an organization to purchase a "turnkey" CBMS than to upgrade older equipment. Turnkey systems are complete computer/hardware/software systems that are turned over to customers in operating condition. The local area network (LAN) that is created by forming a CBMS can be connected to other networks for external messaging. It is also possible to establish a CBMS through a time-sharing service. Deluxe features of CBMSs include the following:

- A broad array of options when using peripheral devices, e.g., copiers, personal computers, and optical scanners.
- Ease of coordinating and tracking group activities, e.g., time management, word and data processing, and scheduling.
- Computer teleconferencing activities and options.
- Ease in finding and handling files via an "electronic file cabinet."

**FIGURE 4.2**

Computer-based message system (CBMS) within a fully automated office. CBMSs run on LANs or through a time-sharing service.

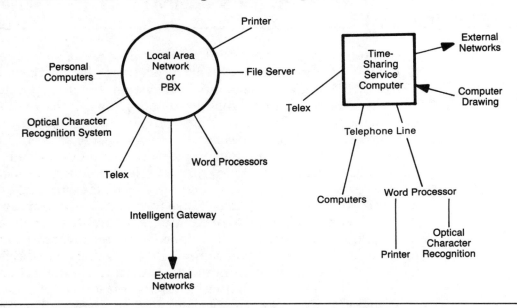

- Directories that include alphabetical subscriber listings, group addresses and names within a specific group address, and personal addresses that give specifics such as department names, titles, mailing addresses, and telephone numbers.
- Ability to function in "real time" when both senders and recipients are using the system.
- A message-prompting system tailored to a particular user's needs and level of sophistication.
- Capability of creating forms (with entry spaces) that appear on the screen.
- Ability to receive mail from or distribute mail to remote locations (other buildings or geographical areas).
- Ability to hold large quantities of information for long periods of time.

**Special Options.** Some EM systems provide a procedure enabling individuals to retrieve messages that have been lost as a result of power failure, telephone disconnection, or other interruptions. Some also provide a procedure that assists users in creating and storing standard forms. Once forms are structured, users need only type information in the blank spaces before transmitting the forms to specified addresses. This process is handy for designing frequently used report formats. In some systems, such formatted information can be cross-referenced and made available to a number of departments within an organization. These capabilities are more extensive within computer-based message systems.

**Savings in Time, Space, and Money.** While both consultants and users agree that personnel can save substantial amounts of time using a CBMS, their estimates of those amounts vary widely. Manufacturers Hanover Trust claims a 36-minute savings per day for its EM users,[2] and the consulting firm of Bolt, Baranek and Newman estimates that users save about one hour a day. On the high end of the continuum, Dr. James Bair of Bell Northern Research believes that time savings can be as high as two hours per day for some individuals.[3]

A CBMS can also be a space saver. By creating a system-wide information database, an organization keeps electronic storage space to a minimum and easily transfers documents among departments and individuals.

A CBMS used to track projects in industry can increase productivity and thus lower costs in the following ways:[4]

- It eliminates production delays by removing obstacles to sharing information and skills.
- It expands management control and facilitates tracking of ongoing projects.
- It expands the range of access to information among team members who are separated by time and space. This permits the formulation and solution of new classes of problems.

**In-house CBMSs.** An in-house CBMS requires: (1) standard terminals, (2) a printer, (3) a local area network (LAN), and (4) an electronic mail hardware/software processor. Additional equipment depends on an organization's needs. The processor can be located in a central computer, in intelligent computer terminals, or both.

In a text-audio CBMS, individuals use a touch telephone or telephone with a tone-generating device to store and retrieve messages that are handled digitally. The system converts the electronic mail to sound or voice that an addressee hears. This system can be very important for people who are out of reach of terminals.

InfoMail™, offered by Bolt, Baranek and Newman, Cambridge, Massachusetts, provides one of the more flexible CBMSs. It is able to link a variety of terminals, printers, and other peripheral devices and to supply companies with all the necessary parts of a system. Bolt, Baranek and Newman operates a large, private packet-switched computer network for users and also makes consultants available to them.

**Successful CBMS Users.** Wells Fargo Bank of California is one of the many companies successfully using an in-house CBMS. What began as a text processing application for 20 technical writers expanded into a network of 375 terminals used by about 2,000 people. According to Wells Fargo management, employees favor the word processing, filing, and calendaring aspects of the system.[5]

The Comet™ CBMS, manufactured by the Computer Corporation of America, has worked well for 3,000 executives and professionals at Manufacturers Hanover Trust.[6] It was first tested among the organization's office automation group, which had special communicating and activity coordinating needs. While using Comet™, personnel discovered a number of unexpected applications for EM. Managerial personnel who previously declined to type their own messages became "keyboard converts." Several departments with EM links began using their word processors and PCs to issue bulletins and newsletters, and a financial service group began to distribute information on foreign exchange rates, commodity spot prices, and other commercial information drawn from public financial databases. The system was so successful that it ultimately required a full-time administrator.

**CBMS Time-Sharing.** When a company finds that the cost of establishing an in-house CBMS is prohibitive, it usually turns to a time-sharing service that has computers programmed to provide a wide range of CBMS services. Most individuals and small businesses that have computers or word processors begin using electronic mail via time-sharing services. Popular among these services are:

The Source™ – owned by Reader's Digest Association
CompuServe™ – H & R Block
Telemail℠ – GTE Telenet
OnTyme II℠ – Tymshare
InfoMail™ – Bolt, Baranek and Newman
Profs™ – IBM

**Using a Time-Sharing System.** When a user logs onto the time-sharing system, he or she is typically presented first with general system announcements. These might include the hours the system operates, the times and reasons it will be "down" (not functioning), and the hours that assistance will be available. The service next displays the number of messages the user has received and the number prepared for transmission. In most instances, typing a simple word or abbreviation allows one to retrieve mail or create new messages. Either a menu or a prompt will request the address before electronic messages can be prepared for transmission.

In all CBMSs, users have the choice of answering messages they have received, forwarding them to others with cover memos appended, printing them, or electronically filing them. A CBMS also allows senders to address groups or categories of people, such as nurses on duty at a hospital station or factory workers on a particular shift who might require emergency information.

Although on most systems users can edit copy and change addresses up to the time they send a message, some systems allow editing up to the time a message is actually read. Courtesy copies can be requested, and users can indicate the time a message should be transmitted and whether it should be delivered as soft or hard copy. Blind copies can also be sent. A CBMS system automatically appends the sender's name and the time and date of transmission when a message is sent.

Automatic alphabetical file directory assistance can also be supplied, as well as the option of changing file names for security reasons. As a safeguard against accidental deletion, an "electronic wastebasket" (file) is kept for deleted material. It can be accessed if necessary.

CBMS time-sharing systems generally include separate files for messages that are sent, unsent, read, and unread. They also allow users to set up and maintain extensive electronic filing structures similar to those found in offices. These are created with the help of menus or commands.

# EM VIA PERSONAL COMPUTER (PC)

Often called microcomputers, personal computers (PCs) function like more powerful minicomputers and mainframes but do not handle as much information or manage it as speedily. As PCs are becoming more popular in business and for private use, the market is expected to quadruple by 1990.[7] Their owners provide an increasingly enthusiastic base of electronic mail users (see Figure 4.1).

Before the next decade, PCs are expected to replace specialized data-entry terminals for storing information in mainframes. PCs will also use mainframes to store and forward messages, and will become part of in-house data communications and data-sharing networks.[8]

When PCs are connected to communications or LAN networks, they can interact with other communicating devices of all sorts throughout the world. "Integrated" PC software provides such features as basic word processing and communications, including EM and teleconferencing, mathematical calculations, and spreadsheet analysis. It can also have the capabilities required to prepare reports, rework data, and access remote files.

Software is also able to provide PC users with an EM host system that can be ordered to pick up and deliver messages from other communicating devices at designated times.

When PCs were first introduced, management information system (MIS) specialists who program mainframe computers and control company information were skeptical about the wisdom of bringing them into the office arena. It is suggested they could foresee the day when executives would use PCs to tap company databases and control company information independently of MIS personnel.

Some objections to using PCs for electronic mail were technically valid. Initially the equipment storage systems were too slow to be cost effective for supporting messaging, and few support products were available to make the required networking an easy task. Today, storage-disk capacity often exceeds 1 gigabit, and speeds are 9,600 baud and higher. These rates far exceed the early 300-baud rates that tied up company equipment for long periods and resulted in high monthly telephone bills. Currently, transmission costs can be kept down by using intelligent modems that store messages until they can be forwarded when rates are lowest.

**Interacting Personal Computers.** As users become acquainted with PC features, they usually demand more functions for their equipment. The following brief tale describes the way in which two bank officers were initiated into the world of communicating personal computers.

Paul Smythe was a lending officer with River Bank, an institution that owned a large mainframe computer. The mainframe stored a lot of information that was of only casual interest to Smythe. As the number of his clientele grew, the managers at River Bank decided it would be economical to purchase a PC for Smythe so that he could store information pertinent to the narrow requirements of his job. The problem was that Smythe, a creative person with no computer background, took an interest in the equipment and began to spend both working and leisure hours developing programs for it. His supervisor felt Smythe would be more productive if he actively sought new business.

In the next office sat Jane Tuck, a second lending officer who had also been given a PC. While Smythe dealt with large manufacturing organizations, Tuck specialized in retail establishment loans. Unlike Smythe, Tuck was bent on making her equipment take shortcuts that would save her hours of work.

Observing the time being lost to the loan department because of Smythe's and Tuck's programming efforts, their supervisor asked River Bank managers if one of the bank's software programmers could develop specialty programs for the loan department. One programmer welcomed the challenge of this job and went to the bank's mainframe computer to do his work. The mainframe had the power and programs to generate specialty programs for the loan officers.

Unfortunately, the mainframe computer used a language that the loan department PCs could not understand. Thus they could not accept the specialist's work. To solve this problem, the programmer purchased a "translator" program that converted the mainframe's language to one the PCs could understand. This enabled the PCs to accept his work.

When this had been accomplished, Smythe and Tuck found they occasionally wanted to access very specific information available in the River Bank computer database. In effect, they wanted to establish micro-mainframe interconnections. The now-friendly programmer told them there were two ways of accomplishing this. The first option was to place mainframe terminals on their desks next to each PC, a costly and clumsy choice. The second option was to establish mainframe-terminal interconnections through a process called emulation. The specialist explained that emulators are equipment that combines hardware and software programs and would permit Smythe's and Tuck's PCs to interact with the River Bank mainframe.

However, once the programmer established their mainframe interconnection, Tuck began to wonder why she couldn't go through the mainframe to access various financial databases that other bank officials used routinely. She was told that this would require stepping up her micro's signaling procedures, a process called a protocol conversion.

By now, the loan officers had learned from friends that their PCs could become part of a local area network (LAN) that would provide them with electronic mail service and permit them to transmit documents and records to other banking departments. So, with the idea of saving themselves steps, phone calls, memo writing, and precious time, Smythe and Tuck pressed the River Bank managers to establish a LAN. When the LAN was in place, management found it could issue employees all sorts of information on the company's electronic bulletin board. It also discovered the benefits of using the LAN to hold daily computer conferences instead of weekly, time-consuming, face-to-face meetings.

The "joys of electronic messaging" led Smythe to improve his typing skills, and he soon began typing his own letters instead of depending on departmental secretaries. Other loan officers followed suit, and before long the department required only one person to handle its secretarial needs. This was just the beginning of the River Bank automation story.

# EVOLVING COMPUTER SYSTEMS BROADEN THE SCOPE OF EM

The development of newer equipment and software enhances the value of electronic messaging by making it possible to send more than simple textual material. For example, ROLM®, Zaisan, and other companies produce "hybrid" telephone/computer terminals that offer sophisticated communications service along with information transmission/retrieval capability (see Figure 4.3). There are also personal computers and teletypewriters that have word processing capability. The Wang Personal Image Computer™ (PIC) combines scanning and text-handling techniques and transmits graphics as well as textual materials to other PICs. In addition to providing electronic mail functions, the PIC:

- Scans, enlarges or reduces, lightens or darkens, or rotates diagrams, photographs, and other visuals.
- Merges images with text for reports or other materials.

## FIGURE 4.3

*The ROLM® Cypress™ personal communication terminal combines data terminal, digital telephone, and other services to provide simultaneous access to data and people. The terminal is linked to a keyboard.*

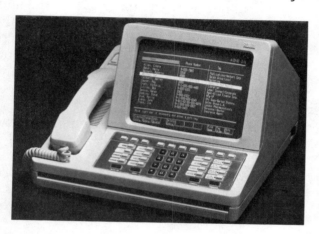

- Attaches descriptions to images.
- Links images to database records and annotates them.
- Files and retrieves images based on their descriptions.

## Optical Character Recognition (OCR) Systems

An optical character recognition system reads and encodes printed alphanumeric characters. When scanned by an OCR system, letters, forms, and documents are converted into digital form. This enables such equipment as a word processor, computer, local area network, or private branch exchange to transmit the information to a printer to be copied (see Figure 4.4).

Computer "add-on" devices currently available also enhance equipment sophistication. The Pixie™ of Electric Data Services Company, for example, scans, digitizes, compresses, and transmits hard copy that ranges from a one-inch square to an eight-by-eleven picture. Ditto™ (Digital Image Transfer and Telecommunications Operator), a software package available with Pixie™,

**FIGURE 4.4**

Optical character recognition (OCR) system.

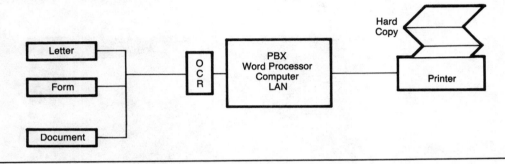

enables the sender to "clean up," edit, or produce special graphics effects as well. DEST equipment provides an OCR system with automatic document entry for word processors (see Figure 4.5). The IBM 7730-Video Conference Unit™ (VCU) that attaches to the IBM PC/XT™ enables the user to participate in slow-scan video teleconferencing.

### Portable Electronic Mail Systems

Besides being useful for people who work outside an office setting, portable communicating terminals take up less space in offices than many desktop computers and are easily moved when employees must share equipment. One such terminal is only one inch deep and weighs just over three pounds. It has built-in communications capability, automatic dialing, answering, and other features. Most portables, however, do not have both sufficient power and the features that people need.[9]

## VOICE MAIL (VM) PARALLELS ELECTRONIC MAIL

Voice mail (VM), also called "voice store-and-forward," is an easy, economical way of communicating when a natural-sounding message is preferable to hard or soft copy messaging and

**FIGURE 4.5**

The DEST WorkLess Station™ provides optical character recognition technology that allows automatic entry of typed documents for word processor communication.

synchronous communication is not essential. Voice mail is entered via a touch telephone, a dial telephone that has a tone generator, or through personal computers that have voice telephone capabilities (see Figure 4.6). This technology is particularly useful for those who do not type and those who like the convenience of dictating their messages. An industrial psychologist warns, however, that some people will resist using VM because they do not like talking into machines and prefer their opinions written down.[10]

Although voice mail accessed through a PBX system is not intended for lengthy messaging and does not have printout facilities, it parallels electronic mail in the following ways:

- It ensures that messages reach recipients by alerting them periodically until they request their messages.

**FIGURE 4.6**

Voice mail on a private branch exchange.

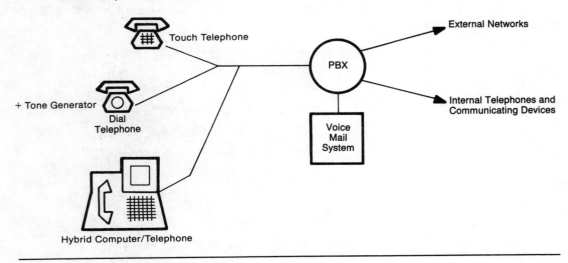

- Recipients can instruct the system to divert incoming calls to other telephones.
- The abbreviated PBX dialing system can be compared to typing a recipient's ID code.
- Gateways to local area networks may be accessible.
- Public or private data network services may be accessed through modem pooling.

**Using Voice Mail.** When voice mail is entered via telephone, the local PBX (private branch exchange) converts the sound into digital signals that are stored on a high-speed disk subsystem for processing. Signals are compressed and reduced to standard signaling rates that are acceptable to the microcomputers that file and store them. Compressing the data reduces the storage space required. These messages can then be edited or stored for future transmission. When an addressee retrieves messages, the stored digital signals are reconverted to their original audio format (see Figure 4.7).

### FIGURE 4.7

The DSC-200 VoiceServer™ is a voice application processing system with voice mail and voice file capabilities. It can be linked with a PBX or key system.

Many benefits of advanced electronic mail also apply to voice mail systems, including asynchronous messaging. The following benefits, however, are specific to voice mail:

- VM acts as a message center, eliminating the need for operators.
- VM reduces the need to write memos.
- VM can be used for dictation.
- Messages can be played back to ensure that they are correct.

A voice mail system is accessed by entering a name or number on the telephone keypad. For security reasons, a password or identification number is used to access many systems. The following features are found in VM systems:

- Voice prompts and/or helpful signals to guide users.
- Choices such as: listen, record, delete, reply, cancel, replay, and send.
- Ability to skip forward or backward.
- Ability to scan, reroute, and file messages.
- Queuing priority for messages.
- Verification of messages received.
- Ability to append comments and forward messages.

Some voice mail systems offer the following additional services. They:

- Accept calls from nonusers.
- Act as an answering desk.
- Page addressees.
- Provide network access.
- Provide control over mailbox features.
- Indicate the number of messages in a mailbox.
- Broadcast to users and nonusers.
- Repeat calls at defined intervals.
- Provide self-instruction and voice prompts.
- Allow users to override prompts.
- Evaluate and administer a system.
- Allow system expansion and upgrading.
- Interface with clients' telephone networks.

There are, however, some problems associated with voice mail systems, including the following:

- High monthly charges.
- Limited editing and no printing.
- Inadequate storage space.
- Limited expansion capabilities because of the PBX system structure.
- Inadequate access lines.

**Examples of Voice Mail Use.** VM is especially useful to people who are located in different time zones. For example, an executive who works for a Beverly Hills, California, corporation but is based in Zurich, Switzerland, finds that when he is ready to close his office and go home for the evening, his California counterparts have just started their day's work. Using voice mail, he can easily tell them about his activities. When he returns to his office the next morning, decisions from headquarters will be waiting for him. This avoids expensive long-distance "telephone tag."

Hoffmann-LaRoche pharmaceutical company uses the Voice Mail Exchange™ (VMX) system to enable its sales staff to communicate with the company 24 hours a day. Its sales personnel call in at their convenience to report on sales performance and exchange (asynchronously) all types of information. Communications might include anything from a discussion on changes in strategy and pricing to questions about technical data. The company reports that VMX calls average about 75 seconds.[11]

Prior to using VMX, Hoffmann-LaRoche salespersons working away from company offices and not routinely stopping at them before making sales calls felt remote from operations. As voice mail grew popular at Hoffmann-LaRoche, other company departments joined the system, and some outside professionals were allowed to use the VMX system.

**Voice and Data Integration.** By integrating message transmission and data transmission within one network, an organization can take advantage of the best features of both types of transmission at the least possible cost. While installing one or the other transmission system separately might not be cost-justifiable, a combination of the two may well be. After business hours, voice circuits which are not otherwise in use become available for electronic and voice mail traffic.[12]

Voice and data systems have been integrated into the following types of organizations:

- Companies that process general business data.
- Companies that have automated to some degree.
- Laboratories, factories, and/or industries using time-process control.
- Establishments that require temperature, lighting, or security control systems.

Local area networks (LANs) located in highly automated factories or laboratories can also support integrated voice/data systems, although the amount of voice traffic they can carry depends on available telephone (tie) lines and disk storage space.

**Supplementary Voice Mail Services.** Studies have shown that large corporations using thousands of telephones are more likely to buy add-on equipment that provides voice mail and can be integrated with their existing telephone services than they are to purchase a new PBX system that gives them access to voice mail capabilities.

Independent time-sharing services also provide worldwide VM services. These are intended for organizations that are interested in VM but cannot justify purchasing their own equipment.

# FACSIMILE (FAX) SYSTEMS

The principle of facsimile transmission was discovered in the mid-1800s, but fax equipment has only been developed commercially and gained popularity since the 1930s. Newspaper wire services have depended on fax for transmitting pictures for many years. Many fully automated offices have retained fax equipment as useful scanning and transmission devices, and some companies find it provides an adequate EM system because it is faster than the U.S. Postal Service and less costly than overnight courier services.

Facsimile machines scan and code graphics, photos, and textual material and then transmit the coded signals to other facsimile devices via telephone connections. The receiving equipment produces a hard copy of the original material. This is an advantage in transmitting previously printed or typed documents, graphics, logos, signatures, and photographs (see Figure 4.8).

Facsimile equipment offers the following advantages:

- It is simple to operate.
- The equipment scans and copies text, photos, or graphics onto the addressee's paper.
- Documents already in use require no special preparation for transmission.

**FIGURE 4.8**

Facsimile (fax).

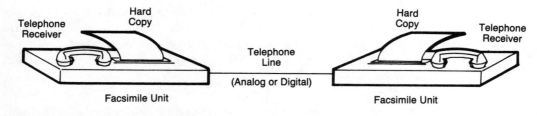

- It transmits via low-cost, conventional phone lines. This is an important consideration because today even the most remote corners of the world are reachable by telephone.
- Transmission is basically error-free, except when line noise or a malfunction disrupts the connection. When this occurs, the result is incomplete copy at the receiving end, and the recipient must ask the sender to retransmit the signals.

**Using Fax Systems.** To use an early fax model (many are still in use), a sheet of paper is mounted on the machine's rotating drum or flat-top surface. The sender then telephones the recipient and asks to have the receiving device prepared to receive a transmission. When the receiving machine's drum has been covered with a sheet of photosensitive paper, the sender cradles his or her telephone receiver in the appropriate place in the machine, switches on the equipment, and begins transmission.

When transmission is completed, the sender and recipient use the same telephone connection to exchange information on print quality. If poor telephone lines and noise (interference) have affected transmission quality and the resulting copy is unsatisfactory, the sender retransmits particular pages.

When a fax machine is activated, the drum spins while a traveling light beam hits the original document. The equipment measures the intensity of reflected light and sends that information over the phone to the receiving machine. That device then produces a copy of the original white-to-black tone range. If a user desires a photographic-quality copy, photographic paper can be applied to the receiving drum and later developed in a photo lab.

Most fax systems today are self-loading and can be programmed to operate unattended. They also skip over white spaces and compress transmission signals, reducing both transmission time and storage space. In addition, current models have store-and-forward capabilities, an important cost consideration. Information can be held, then sent when telephone rates are lower. Some fax models have keyboards for entering text and monitors for displaying it. Hybrid fax models also combine optical character recognition (OCR) and facsimile features. These units "read" print but switch to the facsimile system when an image cannot be identified.

**Features and Drawbacks of Fax.** Although fax systems provide only station-to-station service, newer devices have an important place in the automated office. Advanced Group IV fax machines produce many copies per minute, transmit over lines designed to handle digital signals, and interconnect directly with computers and intelligent copiers. These features are adequate for some organizations' electronic mail needs. Current fax equipment enhancements provide:

- Swift reproduction.
- Storage capability of up to 60 documents.
- Store-and-forward capability.
- Automatic document feeding, dialing, and receiving.
- Security code transmission.
- Automatic handshake – a signaling procedure between machines indicating that each device is prepared to transmit or receive.
- Block skipping – a scanning procedure by which equipment skips those areas having no image or text.
- Error checking – a system for checking the quality of incoming signals for "noise."

Automatic fax equipment that sends analog signals has a serious limitation. Because noise (interference) caused by poor-quality phone lines affects the final product, senders can never be certain of the quality of copy produced at the receiving end. Recently developed fax machines that translate scanned information into digital data and send it via data-grade telephone lines, however, do not usually have this problem. Older fax equipment also has the problem of communicating with newer models and with other automated office equipment. This is an important consideration in environments that are becoming progressively more automated.

Current fax equipment on the market competes most closely with electronic copier-printers. Copier-printers scan hard copy and are able to store the information on it for reproduction elsewhere when requested. The distinction between fax systems and intelligent copiers is expected to disappear over time.

**Where Fax Provides Sufficient Messaging Service.** Peter Pan Seafoods, Inc., of Seattle uses a modern Panafax™ facsimile unit to manage the electronic messaging it requires. The company maintains a network of plants and buying stations from Seattle to the far reaches of Alaska and depends upon good communication and fast processing even when distance and poor weather delay conventional communications services.

Almost all the business needs of the seafood company—from "catch" information and payroll figures to infirmary supply requirements—are covered by fax communications. The modern units automatically query each other for the best transmitting speeds and signals, then exchange vital information between the company's home office and coastal stations.[13]

# TELEX AND TWX

Teletypewriting systems, often called TTYs or telex, are an early form of station-to-station electronic messaging that for many years served as the internal communications backbone for businesses and news services. Because these systems are so numerous and well established throughout the world, they are being upgraded to function in the current communications arena (see Figure 4.9).

**FIGURE 4.9**
*Telex.*

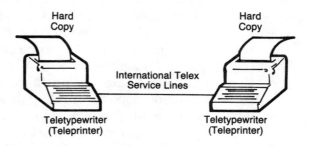

Telex I and Telex II—the latter also known as TWX (*T*eletype-*W*riter E*X*change)—are worldwide teleprinting services based on different signaling procedures. Both systems are owned and operated by Western Union (WU) in the United States. They reach about 180,000 businesses in this country and 1.5 million terminals throughout the world.

Telex users can key in messages for immediate transmission, "punch" them on paper tape, and—depending on the type of equipment—record them on cassettes or disk systems for later transmission.

While teletypewriting has traditionally been a low-cost method of communicating, older terminals—many of which are still being used—provide poor print quality, transmit slowly (10-15 characters per second), have limited character sets, and require open, or end-to-end, connections as in a telephone call. An open connection, however, has the advantage of allowing a series of real-time exchanges to take place without the need to reconnect terminals.

Current terminal models are considerably quieter, and their transmission speed is faster. Both Telex I and Telex II services have also been updated, providing senders with a store-and-forward feature, broadcasting, and abbreviated and prepro-grammed addressing. In preprogrammed addressing, the client establishes lists of addresses with a utility company. These are retrieved and used when the client chooses to send messages to particular groups of people.

Western Union provides a service whereby people can reach its Telex I or Telex II center using teletypewriters, communicating word processors, computers, or telephones. Message-switching computers or operators accept and sort the information and route it on to its destination to be printed. When a message is handled as a Mailgram (a joint WU–U.S. Postal Service operation), it goes to a selected postal office where it is printed, inserted in an envelope resembling those used for telegrams, and delivered as regular mail by a letter carrier.

Other major national networks also have switching centers that accept this type of communicating. The International Telephone and Telegraph Company (ITT) computer network service will hold messages until addressees use their private codes to retrieve them. This enhances the privacy of communications and provides a service that approaches a person-to-person electronic mail system (see Figure 4.10).

## TELETEX

Teletex (often confused with the information display service Teletext, described later) is an international system or standard for transmitting information at 1,200-2,400 bits per second from one communicating device to another.

The engineering design of the teletex system allows it to operate on current communications networks. Thus it can take full advantage of the transmission capabilities of microprocessors and communicating word processors. European communication specialists expect teletex to replace telex and encompass facsimile as the international standard is upgraded.

The features of the system are also intended to encourage the development of electronic mail use by creating:

- International compatibility.
- Automatic message transfer for networks and terminals.
- A large alphanumeric character repertoire.

**FIGURE 4.10**

An ideal network would provide clients with these communications options.

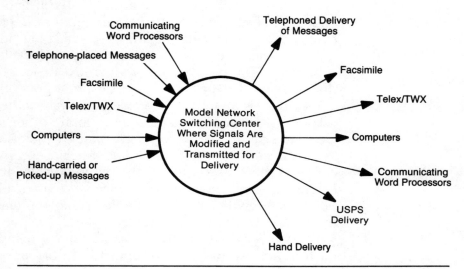

- Transmission controls and protocols with facsimile equipment compatibility.
- Editing and text-manipulation functions.
- Reception during transmission.
- Minimum transmission rates.
- Specified minimum performance rate.

# VIDEOTEXT

Videotext systems transfer information stored at a transmission station to the memory system of a viewer's TV screen. These systems are useful to the mass market of households and small businesses that do not need and cannot afford to access massive computerized database systems. They are also economical because they do not require the recipient to have a computer to carry out their functions. The development of newer, two-way cable TV systems carrying a mix of data, voice, and video signals is expected to enhance this trend.

In time, videotext is expected to challenge the Yellow Pages telephone directory and newspaper classified ad sections and to provide users with complete and updated lists of recreational, educational, religious, and other information. Because videotext can be delivered via phone lines, coaxial cable, and regular TV, many groups stand to profit from its use when it becomes more successful. The proponents of videotext expect each company that advertises to pay a fee for its listing rights.

Viewdata is an interactive videotext system the home viewer can use to order merchandise and obtain other services. Typically, a user accesses viewdata service by means of a television set connected to a telephone line. Special electronic circuitry converts the TV set into an information display terminal, and a calculator-like keypad enables a viewer to control the information flow. Viewdata can provide electronic mail and is being used in this way by the British Prestel system.

The viewer controls the presentation by using ten numeric buttons and two other small controls. Information is organized as an index (or menu) that appears on the screen.

Teletext is a similar system, but it provides only one-way service—storage terminal to viewer—via "over-the-air" television transmissions. Thus viewers who want the advertised services must telephone in their requests.

Listed on the facing page are the various forms of videotext that are now on trial or will soon be tested in the United States and abroad.

Videotext systems use the "blanking space" between consecutive TV frames to transmit pages of information. These are lines at the bottom of TV frames that are used to transmit vast amounts of technical information. Some of these lines can be brought onto the television viewer's screen by the system.

To receive this information, a TV set must be equipped with a "decoder." This device captures and stores information on the desired page and displays it on the TV screen. While the decoder is doing its job, the sending service continues to transmit hundreds of pages of information continuously, in rotation, at a high speed.

| Generic Name | Trade Name |
|---|---|
| Teletext<br>    Service delivered via<br>    standard over-the-air<br>    broadcast television<br>    signal | Info-Text (U.S.)<br>Ceefax (BBC, Britain)<br>Oracle (IBA, Britain)<br>Antiope (France)<br>Bildschirmzeitung (Germany) |
| Viewdata<br>    Service delivered via<br>    telephone or other wired<br>    connection | Viewtron (U.S., Knight-Ridder)<br>EIS (U.S., AT&T)<br>Green Thumb (U.S., Dept. of<br>    Agriculture)<br>Prestel (Britain)<br>Teletel (France)<br>Bildschirmtext (Germany)<br>Telidon (Canada)<br>Vista (Canada)<br>Finset (Finland)<br>Captains (Japan)<br>Viewdata (Netherlands PTT)<br>TVS (Netherlands, VNU)<br>Datavision (Sweden) |

The user finds information through a procedure known as tree branching, whereby the viewer is led from a menu of general information to menus with more specific choices. A subscriber who wants to check airline schedules, for example, will learn from the directory menu the number of the page on which airlines are listed—say, page 31. Pressing keypad buttons 3 and 1 calls up page 31, a listing of airlines and their separate page numbers. American Airlines might be located on page 31-1, United on 31-4, TWA on 31-7, and so forth. The user need only press the third digit for the desired airline schedule to appear. Pressing a fourth digit might further subdivide schedules into morning, afternoon, and night arrivals and departures. In effect, branching provides quick access to very specific information.

The one-way French information delivery system called Antiope is being tested on stations KSL-TV in Utah and KMOX-TV in

St. Louis. Knight-Ridder newspapers have announced a view-data project with AT&T called Viewtron™. The Times-Mirror Corporation, a mass-media conglomerate in Los Angeles, and other newspaper organizations have entered the cable TV industry while retaining their long-standing roles in the broadcast industry.

Despite the possible economic advantages of videotext, none of the existing techniques has thus far made a major inroad in the American market. Investors appear unable to overcome their hesitancy in backing a particular system until they can determine what the market will be and which system will become more widely used. Some of this reluctance can be attributed to the fact that the two major videotext systems were developed in Europe, and adopting them for use in the United States would mean paying royalties.

Because videotext can transmit news as well as carry advertisements, some communications consultants forecast that it will mean the demise of the printed newspaper as we know it. To guard against this possibility, at least one newspaper is buying heavily into videotext service.

All British Prestel cable subscribers are offered an electronic mailbox with an address number and a keypad or full typewriter keyboard. To send messages on the system, subscribers first reach the Prestel mailbox computer by entering numbers on the keypad or keyboard. Numbered messages then appear on the screen. The user chooses from among them and enters the number on the keypad. Those who have full keyboards can create their own messages of up to 100 words. Once a message is entered, the sender addresses and transmits it—again by entering numbers on the keypad.

The computer receives the messages almost instantaneously and holds them until recipients access their mailboxes. Subscribers can also check on mail while using the service for other purposes. There is no limit to the number of messages that can be received, but there is a limit of three messages that can be stored. Features planned for the Prestel system include: ability to message several people at once (broadcasting), acknowledgment of receipt of mail, and linkage to telex and other communications services.

Prestel has teamed up with two British banks to provide a service known as Homelink, which requires using a home computer. Through Homelink, an individual is able to transfer money between accounts, pay bills, and arrange for loans. This service also provides news and commercial information, offers real estate listings and restaurant information, permits people to make vacation arrangements, and lets them enter bids in the auctions that are frequently held on the system.

Prestel's popularity has grown with its expanded services. Customers in Denmark and Belgium are able to participate in Homelink, and plans are underway to extend the service to Hong Kong, New Zealand, and elsewhere.

Videotext is currently limited by the lack of a hard-copy printer that would operate with the system and by the inability of users to form networks. Authors Sam Fedida and Rex Malik suggest the usefulness of a mesh network over which users could intercommunicate.[14]

# AUDIOTEX—PERSON-TO-STATION VOICE SYSTEMS

Audiotex systems, a less sophisticated form of electronic messaging, provide prerecorded, or prerecorded and digitized, voice-delivered information that is stored in a computer until callers press the appropriate telephone keypad numbers. This sometimes requires keying in an identification number for billing purposes.

To date, audiotex systems suffer from limited vocabularies and mechanical-sounding and peculiarly intoned voices. This effect is created because people who are being recorded must keep their voices to a fairly monotone pitch so their speech will seem to flow when sound segments are connected.

MAVIS℠, produced by the McDonnell Douglas Audio Voice Information System, provides commodity prices via audiotex. Some city transit systems are also using audiotex to inform callers of bus schedules. Dun & Bradstreet gives credit ratings via phone, and other organizations offer stock quotes and news in this format.

# ELECTRONIC MAIL VIA
# U.S. POSTAL SERVICE

The United States Postal Service (USPS), alert to the evolving EM challenge, has introduced several services that depend on electronic messaging facilities. It remains dedicated to hard-copy delivery, however. The most successful of these services has been the Mailgram, a joint USPS and Western Union venture.

To send a Mailgram, one calls Western Union and dictates a message to the operator or sends it in from an office PC or tele-typewriter via the Telex I or Telex II systems. The message is then sent to the appropriate post office for next-day delivery as conventional mail.

E-COM, a second but financially failing USPS service, was ordered by the Postal Service Board of Governors to be sold and its equipment leased or sold to private parties. The service will probably continue operation after it is sold. At present, E-COM continues to accept groups of 200 letters and provide stationery for printing the messages, and promises regular postal delivery within two days. Computer users with properly set-up computers can forward their messages to one or all designated postal offices around the country that handle E-COM. Each message goes to the designated post office nearest the addressee.

For organizations without computers, there are specialized companies equipped to handle bulk E-COM mailings. Some also help write and format commercial mail. Companies such as Software Development and Maintenance, Inc., of Fuquay Varina, North Carolina, and Sydney Development Corporation of Vancouver, British Columbia, offer software programs that enable users to reach E-COM and send mail directly from their own computers.

The shortcomings of E-COM include the following:

- Only white paper is used.
- No logos can be transmitted.
- There can be no return envelopes or other enclosures.
- Dot matrix printing, often considered unacceptable for important communications, is used.

Congress and E-COM competitors have complained that the law requiring the Postal Service to base its charges on the actual cost of service was being abused: that E-COM was charging less than it cost to send electronic messages and subsidizing the service with first-class mail revenues.[15] Though E-COM has failed, it is likely that other private companies will take advantage of the new commercial opportunity.

The USPS international INTELEPOST service is a cooperative effort between the USPS and foreign government postal services to transmit messages via facsimile and satellite. Message copies are "delivered according to the service offerings in the particular country." In mid-1984, the congressional subcommittee overseeing INTELEPOST recommended that the three-year-old service also be terminated because of poor management.[16]

## COURIER SERVICES

As an alternative to postal service delivery, a multitude of highly competitive couriers provide a broad variety of services that range from next-day delivery of original documents to two-hour, door-to-door delivery of copies. Jim Seymour, OA consultant, suggests that courier services may actually serve to accustom users to "the charms of instant, cheap electronic delivery of their messages" and arouse a greater interest in electronic mail.[17]

## CARRIERS EXPAND INTO EM DELIVERY

A number of network companies are providing the public with a broad array of electronic mail formats. These are geared to serve people with almost any type of communicating device, as well as those who have none but require transmission of documents and graphics. There is considerable difference in the handling, timing, costs, and delivery (hard or soft copy) of the various services. Where one service is two hours faster in delivering a message, another costs less, and so forth. As the popularity of electronic mail increases, most EM service companies expect to expand the number of features they provide and the geographical areas they cover.

MCI Communications Corporation, a long-distance telephone company, is among those providing EM. MCI is promoting a four-tier national mail service for text transmission. Users pay an annual fee and then are charged only for messages actually sent. There is no subscription fee, and an EM mailbox is included in the service. Registration of terminal with the company is required, although it is gratis.

All four tiers of MCI Mail[SM] require messaging from terminals. Three service categories deliver hard copies of mail within differing lengths of time and at varying costs. Hard copy includes bond stationery, company emblems, and signatures.[18] It should be noted that until such services acquire large numbers of registered, interacting, motivated users, their business remains limited.

MCI registrants owning computers, word processors, and communicating terminals may send EM via a modem and phone to other MCI Mail[SM] customers' mailboxes via Instant Mail, the fourth tier of service. Among the EM facilities provided are an electronic "in box," a "desk" that holds unanswered mail, a "draft" space where the letter being written is held, and an "out box" for messages sent. These spaces are cleared every 24 hours. MCI is expected to add banking services by tying in with an automatic teller service. A user would pay twenty cents for each bill paid or balance checked.

Western Union also provides a number of specific person-to-person and person-to-point EM messaging alternatives. Among them, the company's EasyLink[SM] service offers the subscriber text-editing capability as well as EM communications, abbreviated dialing, and departmentalized billing for message accountability. The system contains protocol and speed-and-code-conversion software that enables people using PCs, word processors, intelligent terminals, and large computers to send EM over ordinary telephone lines.[19] The user can also telephone an operator to place and receive messages.

EasyLink[SM] is advertised as enabling most direct distance dial (DDD) terminals, word processors, and personal computers to interface with each other and with Telex I, Telex II, or facsimile machines that are registered with the network. EasyLink℠ also offers subscribers a variety of delivery options.

After the company verifies the characteristics of the user's terminal, U.S. subscribers can request that either hard or soft copy messages be sent to similar units around the world. Users are provided access to the Western Union electronic mail system, and they can call in their messages or request that their messages be delivered to auto-receive terminals. Other major networks also accept terminal-generated messages for transmission, printing, folding, inserting in envelopes, and first-class delivery. Other selected electronic mail services are offered by Telemail℠ (GTE Telenet Communications Corporation), Dialcom™ (ITT Dialcom, Inc.), and Echo™ (Echo). MCI, Western Union, and ITT offer international service.

## Two-Hour Fax Copy Delivery

Although they have not been successful as major EM carriers, facsimile service companies have been in operation for more than five years. Federal Express, well known as an overnight shipping service, has joined these companies in establishing ZapMail℠, a service that transmits high-quality black-and-white images as well as text and requires no subscription or registration.

At the sender's request, ZapMail℠ couriers will pick up messages and take them to Federal Express offices. Messages are then "faxed" to the Federal Express office nearest the addressee, printed, and delivered by another courier. If the sender brings a message to a Federal Express office, the charge is reduced.[20]

A fax service is particularly useful to people who need fast transmission of legal, commercial, and private documents such as birth certificates and evidence of sales or settlement closings. Digital transmission lines provide customers with quality copies, and the service is able to "broadcast" messages to a number of people simultaneously.

Postal Instant Press (PIP), another fax franchise, also provides service to the general public. PIP charges for telephone time and for each sheet printed. At least one other franchise provides pickup and delivery service, as well as other business services.

## Your Corner EM Store

Electronic mail customers can also go to their "corner" GTE Tele-net Electronic Communications Center and buy a Telemail℠ electronic mailbox. Terminals at the store will send messages for instant delivery. GTE offers E-COM mail service (in conjunction with USPS) and plans to expand its service to 1,200 stores nationwide.

# 5 Network Systems: How Electronic Mail Travels

## NETWORK OPTIONS

Many different kinds of networking arrangements are used to transmit electronic mail. The simplest network directly connects communicating devices such as word processors and personal computers by means of cable or wire. The "host" computer uses an EM software program.

A second type of EM network is created when communicating devices connected to modems are, in turn, connected to telephone lines. The telephone system transmits the message to a distant time-sharing service computer (the host) where it is stored until the addressee retrieves it (see Figure 5.1). At that time, the message again travels through telephone lines to the recipient's modem and receiving equipment.

A third networking arrangement is to connect the communicating devices to a local area network (LAN) system (see Figure 5.2). People who use computer services and LANs can communicate in several modes using EM software: one-to-one, one-to-many (broadcasting), station-to-station, and many-to-many (computer teleconferencing).

## LOCAL AREA NETWORKS (LANs)

A local area network is a sophisticated, high-volume hardware/ software system that connects communicating devices and al-

## FIGURE 5.1

Connecting to a computer time-sharing service.

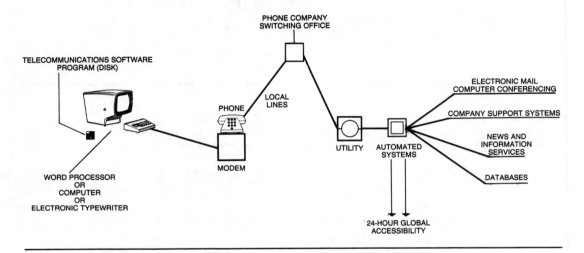

lows them to exchange messages. Depending on an organization's equipment, a LAN typically provides interactive access to:

- Computer data banks
- Electronic mail
- File servers
- Voice mail
- Word processors
- Personal computers
- Video teleconferencing equipment
- Printers
- Databases
- Phone systems
- Telex, TWX
- Facsimile equipment
- Optical character recognition (OCR) systems
- Building management systems

LANs provide an organization with internal communications and electronic mail service, and are cost-justifiable, speedy, and

**FIGURE 5.2**

The LAN ties the office together.

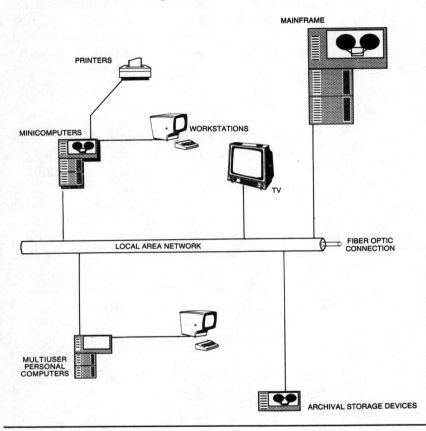

reliable. Although LANs are usually owned by one organization and found in one location, the modular character of a LAN permits it to operate as a single unit throughout a number of buildings, within a campus, across several locations, around the country, or around the world.

The electronic mail processing feature within a LAN can be located in any "intelligent" device on the system, e.g., a computer, intelligent file server, printer, interactive gateway, or special-purpose device. Once installed, LANs are "transparent" to the user. This means the user is not aware of their presence and need not control them in any way.

Local area networks can be expanded or reduced, depending on the amount of equipment that is required on a network. Technical advances also allow people on one LAN to communicate with those on other LAN networks through switch and access gateways that interface with worldwide network systems.

## LANs in Business

During the last 15 years, manufacturers have produced many single-function office devices such as word processors and electronic typewriters that were not designed to interact or exchange information. However, when they are properly prepared and connected to a LAN system, many of these devices can be made to work together and used for electronic mail.

The popularity of LANs has skyrocketed in recent years as managers have come to realize the importance of rapid information exchange for productivity. As a result, the communications industry advocates integrating office functions with LANs rather than through time-sharing services. Studies also reflect the growing business trend towards purchase of software that enables equipment to function as part of higher-level systems.[1]

## Considerations to Make When Purchasing a LAN

An organization planning to purchase a LAN must take into account:

- The number and kind of devices to be connected.
- The distances required between sites.
- The projected volume of traffic.
- The type of accessing mechanism required.

The accessing mechanism determines (1) the complexity of the system, (2) the traffic given priority, and (3) the method used to deal with errors and failures.

LANs can be either custom-made or purchased "off-the-shelf." Digital Equipment Corporation (DEC) cites its successful experience using off-the-shelf products to create a LAN and establish office automation in its Concord, Massachusetts, facility. This LAN has become part of the company's extended network that serves a large part of the corporation's worldwide organization. It was expected to reach more than 2,000 company computer systems.[2]

## Philosophy Behind Successful LAN Use

In order to develop successfully operating LANs, DEC suggests that an organization choose applications that are integrated into an employee's daily work schedule and make jobs easier. Because expansion of a system is almost inevitable once staffs become accustomed to using EM, DEC also advises choosing LANs that will remain reliable even when expanded. It also advocates taking an approach to information sharing that encourages employee participation, providing personnel with account codes, passwords, and terminals so that they can quickly access company information stored on personal, departmental, or organizational network systems.

Through an electronic document server called a Technical Information Exchange (TIE), DEC employees are able to request, transmit, and receive authorized text and graphic material from anywhere in the corporation. Using EM, they then call up a directory of documents and request that particular material be forwarded to them electronically.[3]

## LAN Cable Features

**Broadband Networks.** A model large-scale LAN currently in use in an automated office setting would operate on a "broadband" coaxial cable, insulated wire surrounded by a solid or mesh wire that is also insulated. This type of cable can carry a broad range of signal frequencies that transmit voice, video, and data. While coaxial cable is expensive, broadband networks give LANs the capacity to handle a variety of signals effectively over long distances and at very high transmission rates.

**Baseband Networks.** Baseband networks are a less costly type of LAN that transmit digitized data over shorter distances. They are made of either twisted-pair copper wire or coaxial cable connected by devices called transceivers. Transceivers both send and receive data. Transmission on a baseband network can be extended by using simple repeaters. Early baseband networks employed twisted-pair copper wire for voice messaging, but distortion was often a problem when data was transmitted at high speeds over long distances.

Equipment on a baseband network is bridged to the cable and "acquires" the network when it has a message to send. Information is delivered via packets of data that are addressed to the receiving station.

**Optical Fiber Networks.** Optical fiber LANs, considered the ideal future transmission medium, are now moving into the market. Improved cable quality and newly developed connecting devices overcome a number of long-standing problems with optical fiber LANs and provide significant advantages over metal cable.

Optical fiber is rugged and relatively thin, and operates bidirectionally in some systems. Its cost is rapidly falling and is expected to be less than that of coaxial cable. Simple plug-in connectors used to install equipment are available. The procedure requires about the same amount of time as connecting coaxial wire and requires little special know-how to carry out.

Optical fiber networks operate on very fine insulated glass filaments that range from about 10 to 200 microns in diameter. Rather than transmitting electrical impulses, they transmit light that is emitted by either laser beams for long-haul transmissions or light-emitting diodes (LEDs) for short distances. Bell Laboratories has recently transmitted over 1 billion bits per second on optical fiber cable and has plans for transmission speeds of up to 10 billion bits per second.

Since no electrical current is used in fiber optic cable, transmission cannot be affected by magnetic interference or power surges. This is a decided advantage in medical, scientific, and industrial environments and may also promote its use in the defense industry or other settings where explosive materials are used. A further advantage is that it is very difficult to tamper with optical fibers without disturbing the signaling procedure. Security violations become immediately evident to the users.

## Limitations of LANs

There are many bases on which to compare the different types of LAN networks (see Table 5.1 on page 107). Each type has its limitations. All LANs have distance limitations. Baseband LANs have a 500-meter limit, after which a repeater must be inserted to amplify and retransmit data. The Xerox Ethernet™ baseband LAN is limited to two extensions or a maximum length of 1.5 kilometers. Broadband LANs, designed to use coaxial cable, pick up noise (interference) when extended too far. Optical fiber LANs can be extended only to 40,000 feet through a daisy-chain arrangement of equipment.

## LAN Bridges and Gateways

LANs can be interconnected in two ways, through a gateway or via an electronic bridge. A gateway has the advantage of being able to direct incoming signals to a central pool, whether they arrive by coaxial cable, fiber optic channel, or microwave radio link. When a system sends messages, the gateway is able to review information priorities and choose the most economical route for transmission. Routes might include a private satellite network, a leased common carrier, or a WATS line (see Figure 5.3).

An electronic bridge permits one network signaling system to be modified so that it will work with another. Bridges are useful for managing signals coming in from a satellite transmission system to a coaxial cable system. Because gateways and bridges offer different linkage methods, they are usually combined for LAN use.

## FIGURE 5.3

A switch and access gateway enables an organization to use various transmission methods.

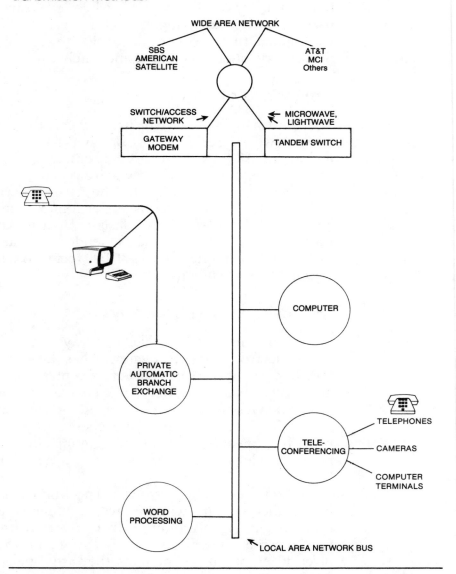

## LAN Configurations

Various local area network configurations vie for popularity on today's market. The question of which LAN configuration is best suited to a business operation depends largely on the organization's physical structure and its priorities (see Figure 5.4). DEC and IBM are collaborating on a study at the Massachusetts Institute of Technology designed to learn how people use 3,000 of the latest and smallest office devices on the three dominant LAN configurations.[4]

Both baseband and broadband local area networks are designed in "bus" configurations in which terminals and other devices are bridged onto a transmission cable to communicate. Each device on a bus carries a unique address code and responds only to messages directed to that code.

A second widely used network design, known as a "ring" configuration, passes messages in a circular pattern until they reach and are accepted by an addressee's equipment. A weakness of this system is that each station acts as a repeater. Thus, if one

**FIGURE 5.4**

LAN topologies.

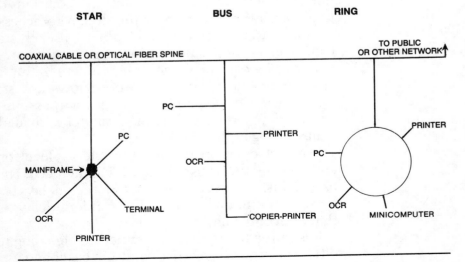

station fails, the entire network is brought down. In bus and ring configurations control can be distributed across the network.

A third configuration, called a "star" network, has all equipment connected to a central computer or switching system that directs transmissions from its hub. Star networks are therefore known as "centralized topologies." A private branch exchange (PBX) internal telephone system is an example of a star configuration. It can also be connected to an organization's LAN.

## LAN Signaling Techniques

Signaling available for accessing a LAN can be broadly classified as either polling or contention techniques. Polling techniques determine the order in which nodes can take turns accessing a network. One polling technique called "token passing" has received quite a bit of attention as a result of IBM's endorsement. Token passing is a means whereby each device, in a predetermined order, receives and passes on the right to use the channel. The token is a special bit pattern or packet of information that circulates around the ring or through the bus. Possession of the token gives the device the right to use the channel.

Carrier Sense Multiple Access with Collision Detect (CSMA/CD) is the most common way to access a network via the contention technique. CSMA/CD anticipates collisions of data and actually uses them as part of the design to access the common channel. "Carrier sense" is the ability of each station to detect traffic on a channel. If a station senses traffic present, it will not transmit its own message. When it senses that the channel is clear, the multiple access feature allows any station to begin transmitting immediately. It is therefore possible for more than one station to sense that the channel is available and begin transmitting at the same instant.

When a collision occurs, the energy level on the channel changes and the transmitting stations detect it. This is referred to as a "collision detect." Each station then delays transmission for a random amount of time. The random delay usually ensures that a second collision is avoided.

It is unfortunate that the numerous signaling techniques, the differences between broadband and baseband methods, and the variety of media and physical topologies of different LAN offerings confuse potential users. Organizations reluctant to commit to any type of LAN usually just postpone adopting a badly needed communications system.

## LANs as Part of a Private Branch Exchange (PBX)

The long-established private branch exchange (PBX) is a natural base upon which many companies can build star-configured LANs. Twisted-pair cables provide a ready-made communications network. Signals generated by equipment connected to the network flow back to a central processor which is the main switching point at the heart of the system and controls signal transmissions (see Figure 5.5).

Digital PBX configurations can be adapted for data transmission and electronic messaging. The ROLM® and AT&T Dimension 85 or 75 are examples of internal telephone systems that can

### FIGURE 5.5

PBX as the hub of the network.

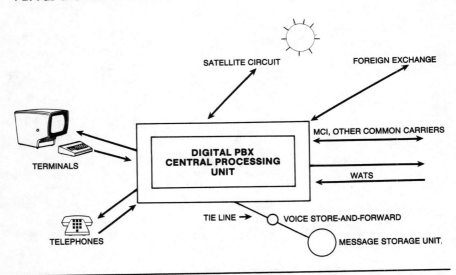

serve as a base for general internal communications purposes and voice mail, as well as for teleconferencing and voice/data workstations.

Whether a PBX serves as a LAN, or a company's internal telephone system is located on a LAN, it can act as a communications gateway to other networks. It can also integrate digital and voice switching internally by moving communications traffic among an organization's terminals and computers (see Figure 5.6).

**Limitations of PBX LANs.** Most digital PBX systems can be adapted to growing business needs. When the capacity of one PBX is reached, "master-slave" or tandem arrangements for additional PBXs can be provided. With the advent of stored pro-

---

**FIGURE 5.6**

A PBX can act as a local area network or be attached to a local area network.

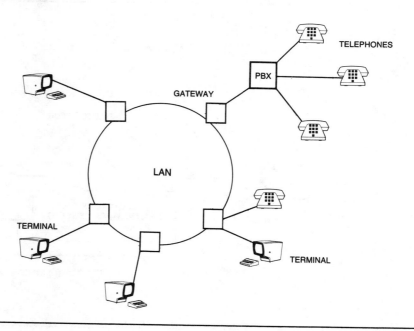

gram control in the PBX system, a communications manager can, without interrupting service, perform moves and changes of telephones with ease. Problems may arise, however, when older systems have insufficient capacity to carry the additional load of computerized equipment without disturbing voice service. Older PBX systems may also be relatively slow in making connections and transferring data. Thus, the age of a company's equipment and its growth expectations will determine the success of expanding a PBX system.

**New PBX Features.** Upcoming PBX features will include:

- Integrated voice/text mail systems.
- Pooled microprocessors.
- X.25 interface (discussed later in this chapter).
- Very high speed interfaces.
- T1 interface (carrying 1.544 megabits per second).
- Integrated still-frame and motion video teleconferencing.
- Integrated applications software of financial modeling spreadsheet systems.
- Vast disk storage capacity.

The PBX and other LANs can be compared in the following ways:

| Characteristics | PBX | LAN |
|---|---|---|
| Simplicity | X | X |
| Lower overall cost | X | |
| Flexibility | X | X |
| Standards | X | X |
| Speed/bandwidth | 1Mbps | 300Mbps |
| (Future) | (10Mbps) | |

PBX systems are limited only by the speeds, bandwidths, and cabling of the telephone system.

A lack of standards in local area network design has deterred potential users in the past. The various standards organizations are, however, making efforts to reach some agreement. Meanwhile, the user community has not had the luxury of waiting for manufacturers to develop standard LANs.

The need for distributed processing and for sharing resources has pressured user communities to adopt one LAN philosophy over another, their choice being determined by the need to service a specific user group. Though IBM has towered over the industry, no compatibility standards for any aspect of LANs yet exist. Some manufacturers have suggested the way around this dilemma is to use "universal" networks. These would add a special module to individual station connections that would enable each device to interact and communicate with the other machines on the network regardless of manufacturer. However, the user would pay a high price for this type of LAN.

### Educational LANs

LANs are increasingly being used in educational settings. Many universities that operate on LANs and use EM internally are connected with other campuses through the Mailnet system, a project of the Inter-University Communications Council (EDU-COM) and EDUNET℠. EDUNET℠ is an international computer service that makes the facilities of 16 academic computer centers available to subscribers. A number of educational institutions that are not connected through Mailnet communicate via major commercial network services.

# ALTERNATIVE COMMUNICATIONS SYSTEMS

Microwave radio, radio and television broadcast transmission, and light link are three additional communications systems that can supplement an organization's internal and external cable networks and serve its electronic mail and teleconferencing needs (see Table 5.1).

Microwave transmissions comprise very high frequency radio waves that are used for line-of-sight communications between company office facilities or between satellite dishes and satellites. Microwave may be an attractive alternative for companies that want to reduce communications costs or "bypass" tele-

**TABLE 5.1. Comparison of LAN Networks and Other Communications Systems**

| | TWISTED PAIR CABLE | COAX CABLE | FIBER OPTIC | MICROWAVE | RADIO-TV BROADCAST | LIGHT LINK |
|---|---|---|---|---|---|---|
| Proven technology | Yes | Yes | Yes | Yes | Yes | Yes |
| Technology | | | | | | |
|   Two-way | Yes | Yes | Yes | Yes | No | Yes |
|   Availability | Yes | Yes | Limited | Yes | Yes | Yes |
|   Maintainability | Yes | Yes | Limited | Yes | Yes | Low |
|   Reliability | Low | Low | Low | High | High | Medium |
|   Expandability | Limited | High | Very high | Limited | Very low | Low |
| Immunity to: | | | | | | |
|   Radio frequency interference | No | No | Yes | No | No | Yes |
|   Power line interference | No | No | Yes | No | No | Yes |
|   Electromagnetic static | No | No | Yes | No | No | Yes |
|   Cross-talk | No | No | Yes | No | No | Yes |
| Bit error rate (BER) | High | Medium | Very low | Low | High | Low |
| Bandwidth | | | | | | |
|   Up to 24 64 KBPS channels | Yes | Yes | Yes | Yes | No | Yes |
|   Up to 50 video channels | No | Yes | Yes | No | No | No |
|   Beyond 50 video channels | No | Yes | Yes | No | No | No |
| Security | None | None | Very high | None | None | High |
| Ability to use system for power | Yes | Yes | No | No | No | No |
| Technical support required | Low | Medium | High | Low | Low | Low |
| Electronics costs | Low | Medium | High | Medium | Low | High |
| Overall system price | Low | Medium | High | Medium | Low | High |
| Worker safety | Low | Low | Very high | Medium | High | High |
| Fire hazard protection | No | No | Yes | Yes | Yes | Yes |
| Impact by weather | Medium | Medium | Low | Medium | Low | Medium |
| General availability | High | High | Limited | Limited | High | Low |
| FCC regulation | No | No | No | Yes | Yes | No |

Courtesy of Cross Information Co.

phone company lines if local telephone companies increase their rates.

Although regular radio and television broadcasting is used for public transmissions, an unused portion of the transmission signal called subcarrier can be used for private transmission of data, audio (sound), and slow-scan television. This is a cost-effective means of delivering training, product, or other information to a number of sites throughout a local area.

Light link transmissions use infrared waves to provide a high-speed communications channel between two locations that are within sight and less than about five miles apart. Because there are no monthly telephone charges or cable installations required, light link is a cost-effective system. Poor weather conditions can inhibit good transmission, however.

### Systems Similar to LANs

Communications networking systems on the market such as Amtel System's Messenger II™ are advertised as operating through the electrical wiring and telephone cables existing in office buildings.[5] Messenger II™ creates secondary, internal communications systems that send and receive telex and TWX and also handle direct distance dialing (DDD) telephone calls.

# NATIONAL AND INTERNATIONAL TRANSMISSION NETWORKS

A transmission network is a communications and computer system that enables senders and addressees to share information. Transmission networks are designed for particular types of traffic and speed of traffic. Because of the tremendous capital investment that networks represent and the technical problems involved in changing lines, network companies until recently have been slow to upgrade lines in response to users' needs.

ITT's international Universal Data Transmission System™ (UDTS) is one example of an advanced vertical network system that uses a very current design standard permitting almost all types of communicating devices to reach the system and be interconnected with databases, data processing and time-sharing companies, and a worldwide telex service.

The CSC/INFONET℠ INTERNATIONAL NETWORK of Computer Sciences Corporation is another vertical network that supplies EM within a fully automated system and encompasses most types of communicating devices. Such worldwide communication companies are referred to as international record carriers (IRCs).

# ADVANTAGES OF ANALOG AND DIGITAL NETWORKS

Networks such as the traditional (analog) telephone system are known as circuit-switched networks. They keep a channel open for communications between a sender and a recipient and have a distinct advantage for EM use. Telephones are available throughout almost the entire world, and telephone network lines have sufficient capacity to carry electronic mail at low speeds during off-peak hours.

Eventual digitization of all telephone networks will also have advantages. Digitized lines accept digital signals fed directly into the lines at high speeds. Thus they provide fast transmission for electronic mail and voice messaging. A facsimile message that would take one minute when transmitted over traditional telephone lines takes only about five seconds when sent over a digital trunk line.

Though there are several types of data transmission networks, all share characteristics that serve electronic messaging well. They transmit information economically and with a minimum amount of noise (interference). They have high transmission speeds and low error rates, and they are "distance independent." This means the network does not charge in relation to the distance a message is sent. Long-haul optical fiber transmission lines used in current networking also speed transmission.

"Hybrid" EM networks combine both electronic message transmission and traditional hand delivery. This combination is useful when recipients have no terminal but need service that is faster than ordinary mail and cheaper than courier service. Western Union's Mailgram is an example of a hybrid system that transmits messages electronically, prints them in the destination area, and delivers them the next day along with the regular mail.

# DIGITAL NETWORKS

There are two major digital network systems, message-switched and packet-switched. Message-switched networks transmit entire, digitized, addressed messages or information as a unit.

Packet-switched networks divide messages into segments—like train boxcars—containing specific amounts of data. These are addressed by the system, then transmitted as a series. Each packet travels independently and follows an individual route.

Both message- and packet-switched networks have computers at network switching junctions called nodes. Nodes "read" the messages and packet addresses, then send them along when space in the information flow allows.

## Packet-Switched Networks

Evolving worldwide packet-switched network systems such as GTE Telenet® and Tymshare's Tymnet™ provide a variety of services including electronic mail. They are particularly useful to international companies and educational institutions that have a broad distribution and different types of communicating equipment. They are also valuable to individuals who rely on foreign databases or who simply want to reach people abroad who have common interests. These networks provide facilities for translating incompatible computer signals so that devices can "talk" to each other (see Figure 5.7).

Large networks can be used by many time-sharing terminals concurrently. Because users generally enter their information for transmission at speeds below system capacity, there are pauses in the flow of packets. These can be utilized for messages of other time-sharing network users.

## Using a Packet-Switched Network

Packet-switched networks comprise data-grade transmission lines, network nodes, virtual circuitry, local database connections, microwave transmission links, and other elements.

To use a packet-switched network, a person first connects the terminal or PC to a modem and telephone line, then dials a local network telephone number to be connected to a network minicomputer or local node. Information received at the node is divided into data packets of uniform size that are addressed and transmitted over data-grade telephone lines toward their destination.

## FIGURE 5.7
Example of a packet-switched network.

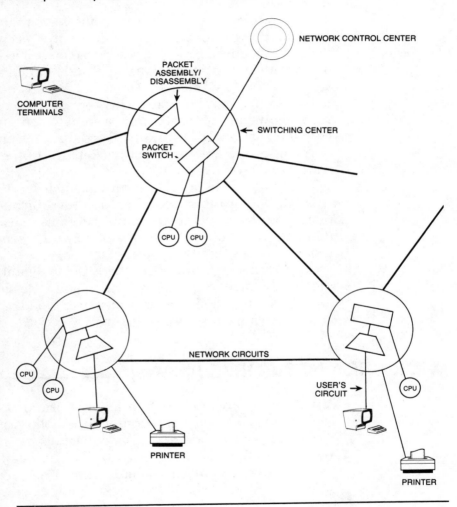

At transmission junctions along the route, nodes examine the packets to make certain their information content is complete. They then seal and route them on to other nodes. At the final destination, packets are sorted, placed in order, checked again for contents, and rebuilt as the original message and forwarded to the addressee's computer. This type of system eliminates line noise and the garbling experienced when voice-grade lines are used.

Nodes function in other important ways that help eliminate transmission difficulties. For example, the receiving node may order a transmitting node to resend a packet if it detects damage or missing information. Another node function is to translate data into a standard format that is universal to all packet networks around the world. This format, X.25 or its derivative X.75, allows any computer on a system to communicate and allows international networks to pass data between them. In addition, nodes are able to direct packets to routes that have less traffic at a given moment.

Today, networks are also improving their service by automatically rerouting messages when a communications line is impaired. Without this feature, interruptions caused by network damage would cause transmission loss, and senders would be required to resubmit their messages.

It is fortunate for those currently using digital networks that the development of packet-switched and time-sharing network lines has come when there is need to use broad bandwidths with great carrying capacity (see Figure 5.8).

## WIDE AREA NETWORKS (WANs)

A wide area network (WAN) is an organization's external communications system. It may comprise a public switched network that carries voice, data and video signals or its own private switched or nonswitched network. The latter can also include a cellular radio system and satellite connections (see Figure 5.9). A satellite station "dish" in the system may serve one or possibly several local area networks connected to it.

This type of arrangement makes good sense when a company needs more than 24 duplex voice channels or one T1 channel (1.544 megabits per second) and frequently places calls to distant cities. Data flows in two directions at once on duplex channels.

**FIGURE 5.8**

Integrating private and packet networks.

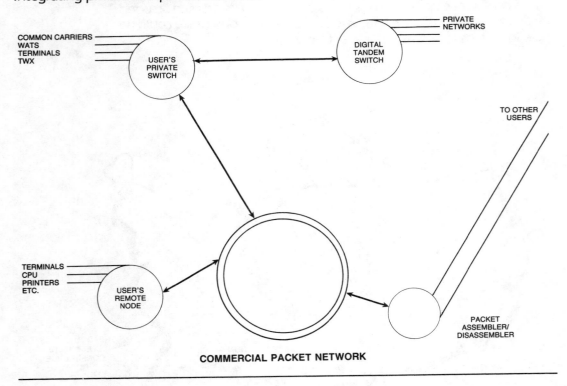

COMMERCIAL PACKET NETWORK

When an organization needs this type of service, satellite time costs compare favorably with those of terrestrial systems. A company that foresees its rapid growth in communications traffic will find owning a private network invaluable.

While it may be difficult for a company to decide on the best all-round communications system to serve its needs, consultants agree that a WAN facilitates communications between any two points on a network and any two devices within a system. With the past as a guide, the eventual standardization of networks and lower-priced satellite stations will encourage the use of WANs.

**FIGURE 5.9**

Wide area network (WAN) transmission. When an organization transmits a conference via WAN, observers at remote locations can respond by phone, computer terminals, and/or video. The conference could be held in various locations, equipment permitting.

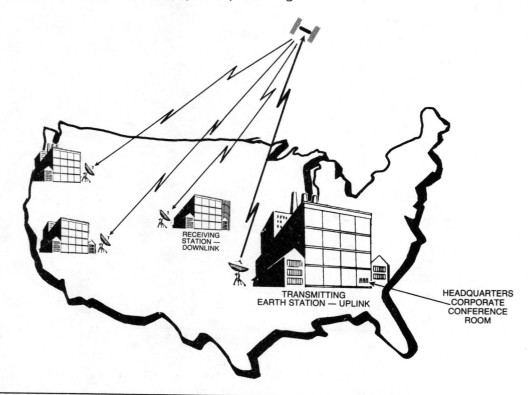

RECEIVING
STATION —
DOWNLINK

TRANSMITTING
EARTH STATION — UPLINK

HEADQUARTERS
CORPORATE
CONFERENCE
ROOM

## Teleports (Satellite Dish Gardens)

Satellites, as part of WAN systems, are becoming an increasingly important part of the general telecommunications picture. Although satellites must be placed in a geostationary orbit (an orbit that keeps the satellite over a specific geographical location), ground stations that send and receive messages from them can be located anywhere within the satellite "footprint"—the area to which the satellite signals are beamed.

Because ground stations can be located almost anywhere, businesses can establish their headquarters in suburban or rural areas where operations may be less costly, wages possibly lower, and surroundings more pleasant. To counter the threat of a large-scale corporate exodus, several cities have encouraged the construction of teleports, or "gardens of satellite dishes," that offer telecommunications links to businesses at a reasonable cost. For example, a teleport planned for Staten Island, New York, calls for 17 dishes and is expected to be completed in the late 1980s.

A unique feature of the Staten Island teleport is that it will be connected to New York City via an underground fiber optic cable. This cable is invulnerable to the weather and magnetic interference and can carry more data and other types of signals than a coaxial cable that is inches in diameter.

"Skynet 2,000" is a plan of Rockwell International, Inc., to circle the earth with 28 football-field–size satellites capable of beaming educational programs, phone calls, and navigational information to people with appropriate receiving stations.

## Teleport Capabilities

Because teleport antennas can handle broadband data, video signals, and sound signals, people around the world will be able to use electronic mail to exchange documents and graphics almost instantaneously, as well as discuss and resolve their problems when they arise.

Business is not just sitting and waiting for teleports, however. Companies like Manville Corporation south of Denver have installed their own satellite dishes to handle client traffic and subleased extra capacity to area companies in need of channels.

# 6 Computer Teleconferencing: From Electronic Mail to Electronic Meetings

## WHAT IS A COMPUTER TELECONFERENCE?

A computer teleconference is a meeting in which remotely located participants access their computer terminals to communicate. They do this in much the same way as they use electronic mail: messages and information are entered into and retrieved from the appropriate discussion files or mailboxes. In fact, a very simple computer teleconference can be arranged using EM messaging, tracking, and filing facilities. Consultants often suggest that companies use their EM systems to hold a teleconference before they consider purchasing computer teleconferencing software.

There are a number of ways, however, in which computer teleconferencing differs from electronic mail. It permits a large group of people to communicate simultaneously (see Figure 6.1). The software program organizes input and channels it to the appropriate people or files. This permits large groups to structure, change, repackage, and report upon information—a particular advantage when problems demand immediate attention and conference participants cannot meet in person.

Strategic planning, project tracking, educational coursework, and projects that involve many people at many different locations, e.g., engineering design projects, can all be carried out easily by means of a computer teleconference. In effect, such a system allows "the right people with the right information to come together at the right time." Sophisticated computer teleconfer-

## FIGURE 6.1

Communicating during computer teleconferences.

PERSONAL MEMO/SCRATCH PAD
ACCESS TO PRIVATE FILES

ELECTRONIC MAIL
ONE-TO-ONE
ONE-TO-MANY

CONFERENCING
LIMITED GROUP

MULTILEVEL CONFERENCING
MULTIGROUP

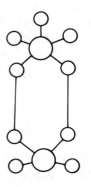

BULLETIN BOARD
OPEN OR GLOBAL ACCESS TO FILE

encing programs such as Confer II™, Micronet™, CROSS/ POINT™, and Telemail℠ are available.

Although some major corporations have integrated computer teleconferencing systems into their management and production structures, computer teleconferencing remains, for the most part, an idea whose time is yet to come. Electronic mail, a subset of computer teleconferencing, is only now being widely publicized as people are beginning to use it and understand its merits. Computer teleconferencing, a more complicated concept with fewer advocates as a result, will probably not "take off" until people have used electronic mail extensively and want systems that will "do more."

## Computer Teleconferences Can Be Held Any Time, Anywhere

Teleconferencing can be carried out asynchronously in "non-real time." That is, none of the participants need be on-line simultaneously. Thus, teleconference participants can come on-line when it is convenient for them and from locations that are convenient for them. Many systems also offer real-time teleconferencing whereby conference participants who are on-line simultaneously can directly access each other's computers. This is comparable to talking on the telephone, although the "conversation" is written text that is transmitted between computers. This feature is particularly useful for decision making in a crisis situation.

## Computer Teleconferences Can Last Forever!

Because computer teleconferences are not bound by the clock or by any one participant's schedule or time zone, "round-the-clock" and "round-the-globe" teleconferencing can take place. There are no time restrictions on teleconference participation, and all computer teleconferencing features are available at all times, including the messaging service and access to data banks. The computer teleconference can be an ongoing, open-ended process, lasting as long as necessary to complete a project—several days, several months, or even (though rarely) several years.

## Computer Teleconferences Save Time/Travel/Costs

People who are key to the success of a meeting can be brought on-line whenever it is convenient for them, thus eliminating their need to travel. When all meeting participants are on-line, all travel and travel costs are eliminated.

Offices that carry out related work no longer need be located close to each other, and individuals who prefer to telecommute or who are homebound can join a computer conference as well as "work at the office" via a home computer terminal.

There is no need to take notes or keep minutes in a teleconference. The system provides a log of conference input for reference when participants want to reconsider facts or positions or when new members join the proceedings. Secretarial labor/costs can thus be reduced significantly.

Projects and activities are easily coordinated and analyzed in a computer teleconference because participants electronically retrieve the same files, messages, reports, and database information regardless of their locations. Thus, people who travel or consultants who are in another location can key into a computer teleconference and contribute their expertise to the problem at hand.

## Computer Teleconferences Manage Information

Vital information is often found in reports that are shuffled from desk to desk, laid aside in manila folders, or waiting in letters to be read. Computer teleconferencing reduces this problem by providing appropriate files that are easily accessed by any number of people who might need the information for making decisions. When decision making is delayed because an organization moves information more slowly than its competitors, its efforts become less timely, less relevant, and less financially successful.

Computer teleconferencing also influences "management velocity," a term that describes the speed and effectiveness with which management solves problems. Figures collected by several major research organizations indicate that white-collar workers spend about 47 percent of their working days in scheduled and unscheduled meetings, and at least 7 percent of their working time on the phone or in transferring information.[1] According to a noted computer technologist, computer teleconferencing systems "allow the executive faced with 'information overload' to produce and manage information more effectively."[2]

Computer teleconferencing systems are used to reformat information flow, making it available on-line to people simultaneously rather than being passed down a list of people one at a time. This helps overcome the tendency among executives to hold onto and control valuable data that could be helping others.

## Computer Teleconferences Boost Morale

Computer teleconferences create team spirit and an element of excitement in group endeavors. Participants who are chosen for their varying viewpoints, backgrounds, and access to substantive material bring a cross-fertilization of experience and insight to the teleconferencing process. This is especially true of the professional or knowledge worker who is known to operate most creatively in a challenging environment.[3]

## Computer Teleconferences Aid Group Decision Making

Conditions that led to the development of electronic mail after World War II also spurred interest in group communications systems. People in business, government, and science needed to cooperatively manage vast and growing amounts of information, to track and control complex projects under development in which numerous people participated, and to hold ongoing consultations with peers and specialists in all fields and at widely scattered locations.

The first computer teleconferencing system, known as Delphi, was developed in the late 1960s by Murray Turoff for the Systems Evaluation Division of the Office of Emergency Prepared-ness in the Executive Office of the President. The purpose of the system was to gather information and to make quick decisions about the then-current wage-price freeze.

The Delphi structure was a carefully designed process of questioning participants, summarizing their responses, and providing feedback on their opinions. The process was repeated until consensus was reached. Subsequent systems brought a number of other elements into the computer teleconferencing process which were quickly applied in business and many other areas.

Today, those at the forefront of teleconferencing research find that groups work more effectively than do individuals in structuring problem areas, generating options, and analyzing results.[4] Mr. Moto-Oka, a Tokyo University professor and chairman of the Japanese advisory council for the study of fifth-generation computers, said of cooperative study in the sciences: "Some new scientific fields have become very complex. To create new breakthroughs, the cooperation of a group is needed. One [person] cannot change these fields very much anymore." Moto-Oka believes that Japan, as a cooperative type of society, may therefore be well suited to make major scientific breakthroughs.[5]

## Computer Teleconferences Are "Meetings of Minds"

When computer teleconferences are well organized, they create a synergy of minds. The computer software structures the flow of communication in such a way that the person who needs information gets it quickly. However, before responding to a request for information, one can take as much time as is necessary to reflect on a problem and come to a decision. All aspects of a computer teleconference are self-paced, permitting participants to think through their contributions and say as little or as much as they choose.

The computer teleconferencing process encourages open discussion and debate, and eliminates certain psychological problems that come up in face-to-face meetings. In a computer teleconference, for example, no one is put "on the spot" to perform or bullied by more aggressive participants. This is often the case in face-to-face meetings where dominant personalities attempt to "run the show" while others, hesitant to put themselves on record, need to be coaxed to contribute. Thus, there is less chance that a computer teleconference will become like the face-to-face meetings depicted by one administrative manager: "a battlefield of personalities, a wasteland of productivity, and a cemetery for unvoiced ideas."[6]

Because participation in a computer teleconference can be anonymous, with status and hierarchy eliminated, people can participate on a equal footing. In addition, the need to write down thoughts in a computer teleconference discourages the verbosity which often annoys participants in meetings. Computer teleconferences can also be used as a means to defuse potential conflict when information is gathered and structured in advance of face-to-face meetings.

## Computer Teleconferences Are Good Management Tools

Computer teleconferences are valuable management tools for coordinating and developing ongoing projects. The system software organizes data so that it supports decision making. People can instantly access the data they need and gather the expertise of others in order to arrive at a decision. Furthermore, the speed, quality, and effectiveness of decision making can be improved because issues can be dealt with as soon as they arise, and statistics and data accessed as quickly as necessary. Computer teleconferences also break the habit of meeting face-to-face, which entails scheduling and travel and limits the number of people who can participate effectively.

Another advantage over face-to-face meetings is that computer teleconferences are open to a wide variety of people who would not normally participate. For example, staff personnel can participate in a computer teleconference that is focused on arriving at significant or high-level decisions. Because staff members are crucial to implementing a decision, it is much more likely that they will carry out a decision once it is made clear that their participation is desired and their opinions count. Participation in the computer teleconference minimally assures that employees have a better view and a broader understanding of company policies. This, in turn, assures improved morale and encourages greater employee participation in company endeavors.

Studies show that consensus is easier to achieve in an electronic meeting than in a face-to-face meeting. Group members can exchange memos and "test the waters" with other participants before bringing issues before the whole group. Automatic polling and voting techniques that are software features make this possible. Quick feedback provided during a computer teleconference can also be used to develop consensus among participants with different viewpoints, promoting better and faster decisions.

Managers should be able to judge when the use of a computer teleconference is appropriate. Some meetings are best held "in person." These are meetings that are emotionally charged or likely to involve conflict, e.g., where bargaining, defending one's position, or persuading others is necessary. Introductory meetings, handling personnel matters such as job interviews or annual employment reviews, or taking disciplinary action fall in this category. One communications specialist, Andrew S. Grove, contends that there is no substitute for a manager's personal presence when it is necessary to describe the way in which a procedure should be carried through.[7]

Information exchange, decision making, problem solving, and goal setting can be carried out in a computer teleconference. Some examples of good management technique that lead to these goals include the following:

- Prioritizing and scheduling activities.
- Development, coordination, and control of ongoing projects such as product marketing.
- Managing the work of a field sales force where company production, inventories, customer orders, and payments must be tracked, filed, and made available to various corporate departments.
- Developing advertising and promotional campaigns.
- Training/teaching individuals/groups in different locations simultaneously.
- Coordinating and developing material written for articles, books, grant proposals, product literature, promotional advertising, training guides, and catalogs.

- Carrying out research on the development of company services, policies, or transition plans, such as moving to a new location or automating a production process.
- Managing and improving production techniques and procedures.
- Centralizing/decentralizing specific company functions.

## Computer Teleconferences Track Projects

Computer teleconferencing software provides filing and referencing capabilities for tracking projects. These projects could range from the development of educational materials for the elderly deaf to the long-term engineering design development of an oil refinery's construction. In the latter instance, files can be created that pertain to subjects such as the contracting of construction work, the progress and costs of that work, and the scheduling of each construction phase, with reports on its completion.

Through computer teleconferencing a corporate engineering department can advise management on the use of stronger, less-costly alloys in producing a popular company product. The department manager can divide personnel into study groups, track their investigations, and integrate information for final presentation to upper management. Group studies can range from analysis of the advantages, disadvantages, and costs of alternative raw materials available, to reports of experiences that other companies have had in manufacturing products that include those alloys. Studies can also cover possible engineering designs and production methods for new product versions, the costs of subcontracting production, and other factors.

## Computer Teleconferences Serve Educators

In academic and scientific arenas, the Electronic Information Exchange System (EIES) at the New Jersey Institute of Technology in Newark provides computer support for numerous public and private study groups that are on-line. The purpose of these computer teleconferences is to serve the needs of specialized study groups and advance the study of computer teleconferencing in general. For example, EIES supported a 1983 international conference that was organized by Canadian and Swedish research groups and included representatives from the Western Hemisphere, Europe, and Russia. The conference was held to explore the topic of cellulose conversion for fuel, fodder, and food, for application in developing countries.[8]

Computer teleconferencing courses have themselves been taught via computer teleconferencing. MATRIX CBMS was used at the University of Colorado to provide teacher-to-student and student-to-student communications, a bulletin board for posting class notices and homework, classroom files for presenting class lectures, and memo files for students to use in preparing homework and participating in class discussions.

The Western Behavioral Sciences Institute (WBSI) in LaJolla, California, carries the educational computer teleconferencing concept further. It has established a two-year course in advanced management processes where, after an eight-day training session in La Jolla, students and teachers communicate with each other from their homes or offices via teleconference.

Computer teleconferencing is of particular value as a continuing education tool in professional areas like medicine and law where states require people to update their educational studies. By providing information on new and unfamiliar areas, it helps protect the professional against problems of liability.

## Computer Teleconferences Go on the Road

Computer teleconferences let people "be in more than one place at a time." J.K. is an international sales manager who cannot be present at many company meetings. His job requires him to be on the road one week a month when things are running smoothly and two or more weeks when problems crop up. Since the international market represents 40 percent of his company's annual sales, J.K.'s input is much in demand at headquarters, especially when marketing sessions are held. Until a computer teleconferencing system was established, setting up marketing meetings at a time when all the necessary participants could be present was a herculean task for company secretaries.

Now, J.K. carries a portable computer on his trips, and he can both travel and be available to management. When he travels overseas and retires to his hotel room in the evening, he rings the European phone number of a satellite communications utility and connects his portable computer to the hotel telephone line. J.K. then dials his company's U.S. computer headquarters and, when he sees a prompting word on the portable's screen, keys in the code that accesses the company's latest marketing conferencing proceedings. Based on a conferencing log that J.K. reads on his screen, he prepares comments and enters them into the log via his computer keyboard. He has become quite successful at being in two places at one time. He feels no pressure to be home in time for management meetings and no guilt when he must be absent!

### EM and Computer Teleconferencing Supplement Other Teleconferencing Systems

The transmission and filing features of electronic mail or computer teleconferencing systems can be used to support audio, video, and other teleconferencing systems. They can be used, for example, to gather electronically filed documents, prepare meeting agendas, and transmit information during other types of teleconferencing. Post-meeting discussion and follow-up material can be collected and distributed. Electronic mail or computer teleconferencing features can also be used before meetings to clear up minor, but possibly emotion-laden, issues, leaving more time for major discussion that can be carried on in a relaxed atmosphere.

## FEATURES OF COMPUTER TELECONFERENCING SYSTEMS _____

Computer teleconferencing systems typically have four operating levels (see Figure 6.2). These include:

**FIGURE 6.2**

Operating levels in a teleconference on upgrading employee opportunity.

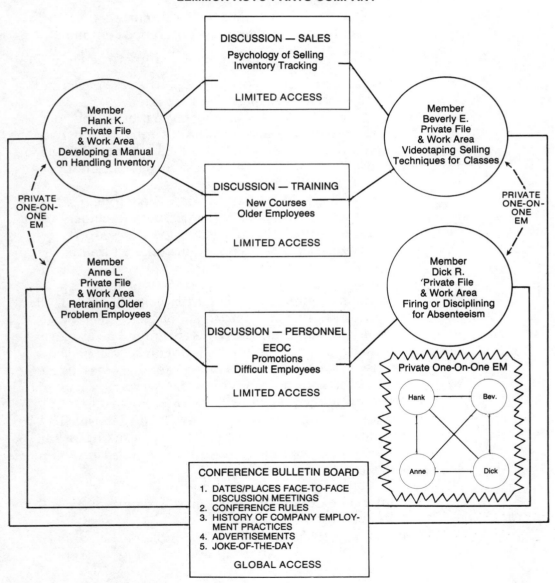

**LEMMON AUTO PARTS COMPANY**

1. a private level for each participant's personal operations and storage needs.
2. a one-on-one electronic mail transmission area.
3. a limited access area for discussion groups assigned to specific subjects.
4. a global area where all participants can access a bulletin board, a log, or general conference comments.

The software provides the following features (see Figure 6.3):

- Private, secure (password-protected) work spaces and files that each participant can access.
- Private, one-on-one messaging (EM) that permits participants to discuss and settle issues and differences of opinion before they are introduced into general conference discussion. Private messaging also permits participants to exchange social amenities.
- A public "bulletin board" file, accessible to all participants, that displays policy changes, announcements of a general nature, ads, advice, humor, and so forth.
- Conference-related messaging, introduced via memos or other formats. Messages are addressed to individuals, to subgroups, or to all participants. In an "open" computer conference, all participants can read all items as well as contribute to all topics.
- Conference subgroup files. This is a limited-access level where participants create material on special projects or discussions. Passwords or access codes may be required for entering such files and serve as a way of structuring the flow of text among participants.
- The "gathering" of electronically filed material. This permits a conference manager to organize discussion, memos, and comments for summary, and provides participants with feedback.
- A directory of participants, their titles, address codes, conference duties, subgroup memberships, place and time they can be reached, etc.
- Broad search capabilities that enable participants to find specific information via: key words or word group-

ings, memo titles, subject, date or number of entry, name of person who created or filed the material, or a predetermined coding or indexing system. These operations are swift and easy because specialized filing and searching structures can be created to fit the needs of subconferencing groups.

- A conferencing log that provides an updated review of accomplishment as well as full documentation on projects under discussion. A log also enables new participants or consultants entering a conference to see what has been accomplished up to that point.
- Voting, polling, and testing capabilities for reaching consensus. Such techniques can be used periodically during a conference to keep topic development on track and to determine if participants have a clear understanding of conference goals. These procedures allow secret roll calls and true/false and multiple-choice questionnaires to be used.
- Availability of on-line, real-time meetings.
- A tracking system that enables participants to keep abreast of new developments and messages.
- A management report system that lets members know how long they have been working at an activity and the associated communication times/charges.

# USING A COMPUTER TELECONFERENCING SYSTEM

To hold a computer teleconference, participants send material developed within their private electronic working areas to other participants via electronic mail. The material may be presented as a memo or document and placed in discussion or conference files, or posted as a general message on a conference bulletin board (file).

One's participation in a computer teleconference is delineated through selective messaging, using passwords for accessing specific group discussion files, and by polling and voting privileges.

## FIGURE 6.3

Matrix transaction exchange (MTX), Cross Information Company.

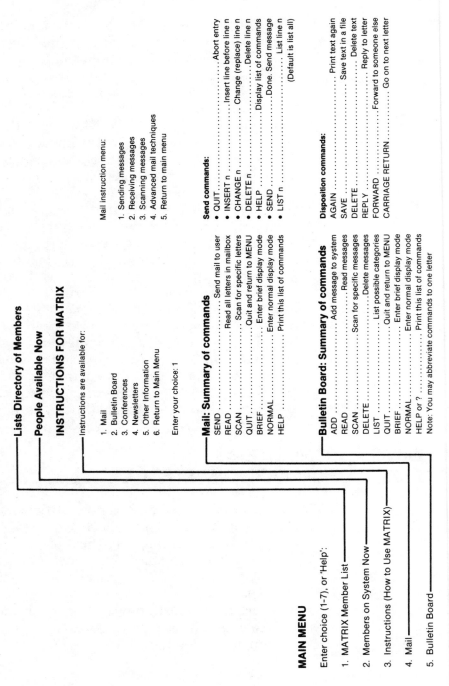

**MAIN MENU**

Enter choice (1-7), or 'Help':

1. MATRIX Member List
2. Members on System Now
3. Instructions (How to Use MATRIX)
4. Mail
5. Bulletin Board

**Lists Directory of Members**

**People Available Now**

**INSTRUCTIONS FOR MATRIX**

Instructions are available for:

1. Mail
2. Bulletin Board
3. Conferences
4. Newsletters
5. Other Information
6. Return to Main Menu

Enter your choice: 1

**Mail: Summary of commands**

| | |
|---|---|
| SEND | Send mail to user |
| READ | Read all letters in mailbox |
| SCAN | Scan for specific letters |
| QUIT | Quit and return to MENU |
| BRIEF | Enter brief display mode |
| NORMAL | Enter normal display mode |
| HELP | Print this list of commands |

**Bulletin Board: Summary of commands**

| | |
|---|---|
| ADD | Add message to system |
| READ | Read messages |
| SCAN | Scan for specific messages |
| DELETE | Delete messages |
| LIST | List possible categories |
| QUIT | Quit and return to MENU |
| BRIEF | Enter brief display mode |
| NORMAL | Enter normal display mode |
| HELP or ? | Print this list of commands |

Note: You may abbreviate commands to one letter

Mail instruction menu:

1. Sending messages
2. Receiving messages
3. Scanning messages
4. Advanced mail techniques
5. Return to main menu

**Send commands:**

| | |
|---|---|
| • QUIT | Abort entry |
| • INSERT n | Insert line before line n |
| • CHANGE n | Change (replace) line n |
| • DELETE n | Delete line n |
| • HELP | Display list of commands |
| • SEND | Done. Send message |
| • LIST n | List line n |
| | (Default is list all) |

**Disposition commands:**

| | |
|---|---|
| AGAIN | Print text again |
| SAVE | Save text in a file |
| DELETE | Delete text |
| REPLY | Reply to letter |
| FORWARD | Forward to someone else |
| CARRIAGE RETURN | Go on to next letter |

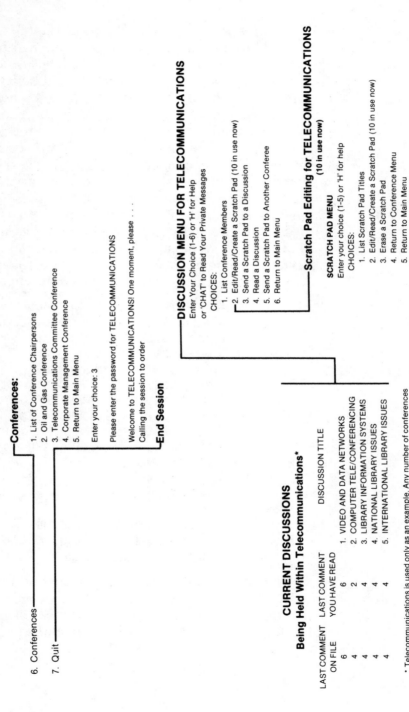

**Conferences:**

1. List of Conference Chairpersons
2. Oil and Gas Conference
3. Telecommunications Committee Conference
4. Corporate Management Conference
5. Return to Main Menu

Enter your choice: 3

Please enter the password for TELECOMMUNICATIONS

Welcome to TELECOMMUNICATIONS! One moment, please . . .
Calling the session to order

**End Session**

6. Conferences
7. Quit

**DISCUSSION MENU FOR TELECOMMUNICATIONS**

Enter Your Choice (1-6) or 'H' for Help
or 'CHAT' to Read Your Private Messages
CHOICES:

1. List Conference Members
2. Edit/Read/Create a Scratch Pad (10 in use now)
3. Send a Scratch Pad to a Discussion
4. Read a Discussion
5. Send a Scratch Pad to Another Conferee
6. Return to Main Menu

**Scratch Pad Editing for TELECOMMUNICATIONS**
(10 in use now)

**SCRATCH PAD MENU**

Enter your choice (1-5) or 'H' for help
CHOICES:

1. List Scratch Pad Titles
2. Edit/Read/Create a Scratch Pad (10 in use now)
3. Erase a Scratch Pad
4. Return to Conference Menu
5. Return to Main Menu

Specifications and features subject to change without notice.

**CURRENT DISCUSSIONS**
**Being Held Within Telecommunications***

| LAST COMMENT ON FILE | LAST COMMENT YOU HAVE READ | DISCUSSION TITLE |
| --- | --- | --- |
| 6 | 6 | 1. VIDEO AND DATA NETWORKS |
| 4 | 2 | 2. COMPUTER TELE/CONFERENCING |
| 4 | 4 | 3. LIBRARY INFORMATION SYSTEMS |
| 4 | 4 | 4. NATIONAL LIBRARY ISSUES |
| 4 | 4 | 5. INTERNATIONAL LIBRARY ISSUES |

* Telecommunications is used only as an example. Any number of conferences may occur simultaneously. The system can be modified to accommodate more than five discussions or ten scratchpads.

Voting and polling are a vital part of the teleconferencing system. When polls are taken, participants can be provided with automatic analysis and feedback—a helpful step toward developing group consensus. Participants can belong to several subconferences concurrently. This is useful when topics overlap and different groups can productively share information.

To participate in a computer teleconference, each person obtains a membership name and password from the teleconference manager. Once members have logged on with name and password, the system notifies them of material that has been entered since they last participated. It then presents a menu of options from which the user can make a selection and which helps the user move step by step through the teleconference process.

For ease of use, most systems allow participants to type in abbreviated commands or numbers. The following messaging choices are typical of computer teleconference systems:

```
 1. CM - CREATE AND SEND MESSAGE
 2. RM - READ AND RESPOND TO MESSAGE
 3. SO - SEND OPERATIONS
 4. ML - MESSAGE LISTING
      A. LA - LIST ALL MESSAGES
      B. LN - LIST NEW MESSAGES
      C. LR - LIST READ MESSAGES
      D. LU - LIST UNREAD MESSAGES
      E. LS - LIST SENT MESSAGES NOT YET READ
      F. RE - RETURN TO MAIN MENU
 5. UM - UPDATE MESSAGE
 6. DM - DELETE MESSAGE
 7. SW - SWITCH MAILBOX
 8. GM - GATHER MESSAGES
 9. UP - UPDATE MESSAGE PASSWORD
10. MI - MESSAGE INSTRUCTIONS
11. RE - RETURN TO MAIN MENU
```

Participants introduce information on topics under discussion by entering a memo, statement, document, or electronically prepared format that is called up on a monitor, filled in, and filed for later access. Once information is introduced into discussion, it can be changed or reorganized.

# ORGANIZING A COMPUTER TELECONFERENCE

Every meeting is, of course, organized for a purpose, and meeting objectives are best accomplished when high-quality communication takes place. The teleconference manager must adequately guide the proceedings, or people will tend to blame the technology and conclude that it is impossible to hold a good meeting by computer teleconferencing.

The teleconference manager must also make participants feel comfortable in teleconferencing, or they may fear that the technology will have an impersonal, dehumanizing effect. Once people participate in a computer teleconference, however, they usually comment on how "close" they feel to other teleconference participants.

Without strong leadership, computer teleconferencing can face the same problems as in-person meetings. It is active leadership and membership participation that determine the quality of the outcome. A computer teleconference manager should:

- Set the agenda.
- Determine the length of time the conference will be held and time limits for filing contributions.
- Determine the tasks that discussion subgroups will handle.
- Appoint facilitators who will lead discussion at remote sites.
- Outline procedures for adding or deleting material.
- Set up a bulletin board and choose the bulletin board editor.

All aspects of a computer conference, including the roles, objectives, and time frames, can be reviewed and revised at any time. As in face-to-face meetings, procedures can be monitored as necessary, and discussion subgroups can be created. Information can also be cross-filed and reindexed according to a revised system. Participants are not normally permitted to change or edit files that others have created. It is advisable, however, for teleconference leaders to give at least one participant the authority to add, delete, and consolidate text.

Besides making formal arrangements for the teleconference, the manager is responsible, above all, for the flow and quality of discussion that takes place. He or she must be certain that enough people with appropriate backgrounds are available to cover the topics under consideration so that discussion will be clearly focused. Managers must also ensure that there is sufficient rapport among the subconferencing groups so participants will interact effectively. If necessary, the teleconference manager can assign pseudonyms to participants. This encourages participants to speak openly, and without deference to the status of other members.

Managers should be prepared to guide participants and give them relevant feedback. They are responsible for connecting the threads of discussion and summarizing points as the discussion proceeds. A checklist for the computer teleconference manager includes the following:

- Keep discussion on track.
- Set time limits on discussion.
- Keep meeting objectives at the forefront of discussion.
- Appoint discussion leaders to facilitate discussion in subconferences.
- Make sure that each conferee actually participates by asking questions and/or by asking for opinions.
- Clarify and evaluate the points that are made (not the people) by carefully reading and analyzing each person's input.
- Explain divergent opinions impartially.
- Search for areas of possible consensus.
- When conflict and "hidden agendas" surface, suggest that they be handled in a subconference discussion.
- Summarize input and provide teleconference results to participants.

Because there are no visual or audio cues available to people during a computer teleconference, it is a good idea to prepare and disseminate graphics beforehand. Participants should also be asked ahead of time to communicate as informally as they would like, but to do so with tact. As in all electronic messaging, there is a tendency during computer teleconferences for people to misinterpret terse and ambiguous messages and to respond angrily. This response, called "flaming," is discussed in Chapter 7.

# AUDIO TELECONFERENCING

Audio teleconferencing means holding a meeting by using a telephone system or dedicated network. This popular, real-time alternative to computer conferencing provides a universally available, low-key, efficient type of communicating that is easy to understand and use. The quality of sound must be satisfactory, however, and the text and graphics associated with the meeting made available to participants beforehand or during discussion. Northern Telecom, Inc., and Contech Corporation are two of many suppliers of sophisticated audio teleconferencing equipment.

The simplest supplementary electronic messaging system used to enhance audio conferencing meetings is facsimile. Fax copies are sent before or after an audio teleconference or on a second telephone line during the conference.

Computers and communicating word processors are also used to transmit text and graphics during an audio conference. Information typed into either device is sent through a telephone or dedicated line to compatible equipment and displayed on a video monitor or video projector connected to the terminal, or printed.

A very large part of business conferencing can be covered by audio teleconferencing. It is as effective as most face-to-face meetings for routine consultation and for crisis management, as long as the number of participants and the amount of information handled are limited.

The fields of engineering, law, advertising, and building construction have successfully used audio teleconferencing for many years. Its application in corporations is also well known for:

- Coordinating administrative affairs.
- Interfacing with field offices.
- Training field personnel.
- Coordinating remote manufacturing and construction operations.
- Handling corporate relations.

While audio teleconferencing is practical and comes closer to the face-to-face meeting experience than computer conferencing, it lacks the flexibility inherent in asynchronous communications systems such as electronic mail and has certain other problems. When it is not very carefully managed, it is considered more vulnerable to breakdown than other teleconferencing systems. For this reason, the Kellogg Communications Corporation and other companies provide experienced trainers and educators to work with clients in learning to use audio teleconferencing services.

## Establishing an Audio Teleconference

An audio teleconference can be established in various ways. A manager can use a "call conferencing" feature, dialing all participants directly and bringing them on line. Or, on request, a telephone company or service bureau operator will assist in establishing a meeting. The procedure requires that each conferee be called and placed on hold. Then, when all parties are on-line, they are joined sequentially. However, unless a service organization provides technical support, there will be no assistance when a conferee is accidentally cut off or when there are line difficulties.

An audio conference can also be arranged by conferees dialing a "meet-me bridge" telephone number. This arrangement can be managed through an office PBX, key system, or other networking arrangement. When a meeting is managed this way, participants call an access code number that connects them to the bridge where other conferees are conducting their meeting.

Modern PBX and key systems provide high-quality internal conferencing and allow users to initiate three-way internal and external audio conference calls. There are also specialized computer systems that connect conferees via satellite transmission, bypassing local telephone company lines. Messages travel encoded point-to-point or point-to-multipoint.

Older PBX and key audio conferencing systems, many of which are still in operation, lack billing and recording facilities, as well as equipment to control volume. Because they allow only limited external participation and operator assistance, participants face difficulties in reconnecting people who have become disconnected.

# SLOW-SCAN VIDEO
# TELECONFERENCING FACILITIES

Slow-scan (also called freeze-frame) video teleconferencing is another telecommunications process that is effectively supplemented by electronic mail or computer teleconferencing systems as described above. It is a relatively low-cost system used where images are of prime importance, but full-motion movement is not required. The system preserves to a degree the personal relationship found in face-to-face meetings by bringing the visual element into play, and graphic or pictorial information can be transmitted to unlimited numbers of people at several locations.

In slow-scan teleconferencing, a television camera picks up the image. A scan converter then compresses the bandwidth of the signal and extends its delivery time, and a modem converts the signal to an audio frequency for transmission over conventional telephone lines. A second, parallel telephone connection carries voice transmission.

The receiving station must have equivalent facilities, a TV monitor on which to view the incoming picture, and a speaker for audio transmission. The result is transmission of a TV image that changes about twice a minute (depending on the system) instead of 60 times each second, as in full-motion TV.

When people at several locations need to study an image for an extended period of time, an accessory known as a "frame grabber" enables the operator to store images on the monitor for later use or archiving. The system also allows pre-recorded images on a disk or videocassette to be brought up in slide-projector fashion on either the sending or receiving end of a transmission.

Although some people object to the still-frame presentation of slow-scan delivery, the technique is well suited to teaching at all levels, and to communicating with handicapped or geographically isolated people. Students and teachers feel they are interacting when they can see one another—regardless of the intervening distance.

Slow-scan communication has also proved to be effective when used in engineering meetings where specialists at different locations must determine the cause of product failure and suggest construction changes. It is also especially helpful to doctors at remote locations who must consult with specialists in major medical centers and to medical institutions that broadcast programs on advanced medical procedures or diagnostic techniques. Among many possibilities, the system permits transmission of a patient's image during emergency situations, computerized image analysis, and assistance in the construction of prosthetic devices.

# VIDEO TELECONFERENCING (VTC)

Full-motion video teleconferencing is a relatively new and valuable business tool that comes closest of the various teleconferencing systems to creating the atmosphere of a face-to-face meeting. Although some users claim VTC meetings don't feel "quite natural," most people say they communicate better when they see the speaker. Electronic mail and computer teleconferencing are also useful adjuncts in structuring and transmitting textual or graphic material for VTCs.

Although a VTC system requires a much greater capital commitment than other teleconferencing systems and incurs larger ongoing overhead and maintenance costs, organizations employing such a system will benefit because of:

- High user acceptance.
- Convenience and efficiency.

- Impact.
- Broad range of applications.
- Rapid convening and decision making among participants at widely dispersed locations.
- Improved access to people.

Devices are currently available that modify technology to produce systems that fall between full-motion video and slow-scan teleconferencing. These systems are faster than slow-scan, although there remains a noticeable adjustment to movement. Thus, they are most effective when motion is minimal, as during meetings where participants remain seated and graphics or charts are presented.

# PART THREE

# Integrating Electronic Mail Successfully

How can electronic mail be successfully introduced and integrated into an organization? What is the consultant's role? When should a pilot project be carried out? How do workers typically respond when they are introduced to a new communications system? What are some problems that people have communicating via electronic mail? How do we know which system to purchase? How can we evaluate the system we have purchased?

# 7

## Introducing and Integrating Electronic Mail into the Office

The organization that plans to integrate electronic mail into its office operations will be searching for the most appropriate, easy-to-use, simple-to-maintain, and cost-effective EM system. Key to the system's success will be that it is technically appropriate, well introduced, and integrated into the organization's operation. Because implementing any new technology means asking people to change the way they do things, it is important that everyone affected be properly introduced to the new EM system.

## MANAGERS' CONCERNS

Some managers express concern that they will not be able to handle the new tools, match the equipment to their companies' goals, or sell the operating concepts to their staffs. They sometimes also doubt that time saved using EM can be redirected efficiently enough to warrant the investment, implementation costs, and changes that a new system entails.

In addition, those receiving electronic mail may initially demand hard copies of their messages because they have always received mail this way. When personnel expect paper printouts of their messages, both employee time and paper are wasted.

Another management worry is that EM will disrupt company relationships and that subordinates will bypass the chain of command to communicate directly with upper management. While lower-level employees have always found the means to skirt their superiors when they have wanted to do so, there is no indication that EM is being used in this way.

## WHAT STEPS TO FOLLOW

In general terms, introducing and integrating electronic mail into the office includes carrying out an appropriate implementation strategy, selecting the architecture for it, choosing a particular system, and running a pilot project.[1] More specifically, the following steps should be taken:

- Establish upper management's support for EM implementation.
- Choose experienced, appropriate consultants.
- Determine the specific goals of a proposed system.
- Analyze the communications and information-flow patterns of the organization and employees' attitudes toward automation to determine how a new system would affect them. (See Chapter 8 for auditing and evaluating EM systems.)
- Investigate potential EM system capabilities.
- Initiate pilot projects.
- Discover how a new EM system can substitute for, simplify, or eliminate tasks.
- Prepare for equipment purchase or lease.
- Build a foundation of users.
- Train personnel.
- Apply successful communication techniques.
- Evaluate the way in which EM is being used.
- Follow up on system implementation.

## UPPER MANAGEMENT'S ROLE

It is crucial that those responsible for implementing an EM system have not only the full understanding and support of upper management but also its participation, if possible. This means securing management's early commitment to the study, installation, and use of the proposed system. Arguments most likely to convince management of the value of electronic mail include the following:

- EM increases the scope of an organization's information and communications flow. More people, expertise, and data can be included in decision-making processes.
- EM speeds up communication and reduces the time required to make decisions.
- EM increases overall productivity and saves money.
- EM decreases travel costs and management "downtime." Downtime refers to those hours when equipment is unavailable or when employees are on the road, playing telephone tag, or traveling to meetings.

A manager who actively supports the idea of electronic mail creates enthusiasm among users and expands the base of users. This is illustrated by the experience of Westinghouse Corporation in Pittsburgh. When 70 high- and mid-level managers supported the introduction of EM into the company, 400 additional employees asked to join the system within a year. In 1983 there were 3,700 people using the Westinghouse system, and an average of 150 people each month requesting to be given access to it.[2]

# IMPORTANCE OF THE CONSULTANT'S ROLE

Organizations that do not hire consultants to help them choose and implement an electronic mail system very often wind up with inadequate equipment, inflexible systems, personnel problems, and some financial loss.

Without a consultant's guidance, managers usually appoint employees with limited technical backgrounds to "see what equipment is out there." The problem is that the inexperienced person tends to choose equipment that supports the organization's current, rather than future, office procedures and fails to choose a system which can be expanded. Such organizations also frequently use underqualified people to make final leasing or purchasing arrangements. This can also be costly to the organization.

Most organizations require systems that are flexible enough to be expanded as the company grows. The Bank of America's electronic messaging system, established in the early 1970s, has proved to be a model of flexibility. It now supports a worldwide network of satellite and advanced high-speed communications links.[3] Thus, the loan committee of its San Francisco World Banking Division is able to almost instantaneously transmit loan decisions and exchange letters of credit among the bank's widespread geographic divisions.

Another good reason for an organization to hire outside consultants is that even when an EM system is successfully implemented, personnel who fear that the introduction of new technology will disturb existing communications and authority patterns frequently become hostile to those who have been involved in the selection process.

Given the above reasons, plus the variety of technically complex equipment on the market today, it is essential that organizations retain the advice of experienced consultants. About 5 percent of moneys budgeted for EM should be used for consulting costs. The consultant should be available to answer questions about such relevant areas as:

- Interactive (communicating) devices
- Hardware, modems, and cable
- Software programs
- Storage possibilities
- Networks and configurations available for EM systems
- EM implementation and adaptation
- Users' experiences with systems

Specialists can also give invaluable assistance on such practical issues as terms of equipment purchase or contract leases, warranties, and back-up service. They are familiar with vendor lead times, training programs, and the appropriate questions to ask when calling a user reference list to check on system performance.

After an analysis of the organization's current and projected future communications patterns, the consultant should determine the specific goals of a new system. With these in mind, he or she is responsible for guiding the choice of equipment and system design, arranging a demonstration of the recommended system, and submitting to management a written report that clarifies the particulars of any prospective system design and the networking possibilities. Feasible alternatives for the design and networking should also be outlined. Furthermore, the report should contain projected costs and return on investment, as well as suggest the best ways in which personnel can use the system.

When an organization has leased or purchased equipment and has it in place, expertise is usually also required to modify office procedures so that they will match equipment capabilities and so that new employee work standards can be set. Failure to set new work standards that everyone understands creates inefficiency and will multiply an organization's costs.[4]

## THE "SOFT SIDE" OF IMPLEMENTATION

Every organization should investigate the nontechnical issues that affect the performance of an electronic mail system. A communications consultant can best explain how specific factors will affect the messaging operation. Because every organization transmits material of a different character and importance, these factors should include the type of subject matter to be handled and an organization's communications objectives— whether they are increased sales, increased production, or the development of educational materials.

An organization's communications are also affected by its leadership and operating style, e.g., the degree to which tasks are centralized or decentralized, the formality with which people operate, and the way in which managers monitor operations.

An expert can also coach management on how to retrain personnel who have difficulty adjusting to new procedures. The quality and number of training sessions necessary to implement a particular system should be discussed at this time, as well as the choice of pilot projects and the way they will be managed and evaluated. Discussion should also include individual responsibilities in communicating and the format and etiquette of messaging that will be expected, particularly when specialized materials are handled, transmissions are encoded, or additional responsibilities are required of those who receive messages.

An organization's key personnel should be encouraged to attend seminars to gain "hands-on" experience with different electronic mail systems. A number of companies throughout the country provide this service.[5] Personnel interested in electronic mail should be encouraged to ask questions about prospective systems, and a telephone number should be made available so that everyone's questions can be answered. Managers who encourage questions and show appreciation and support for EM users will find that employees readily accept the new communications system.

Managers should be cautioned that some electronic mail features that appear to be advantages can create serious problems when they are not well controlled. For example, messaging systems that enable people to send quantities of information appear to provide them with a decided advantage. But too much information—unless it is well structured—overwhelms rather than clarifies. And unless a system has unlimited capabilities for managing, filing, and storing information, a recipient may feel deeply frustrated.

## PILOT PROJECTS

Pilot projects familiarize personnel with electronic mail, allowing them to become acquainted with the system and use its facilities without feeling they are taking risks or endangering their positions. People often find creative applications for a system when they are "playing" with it.

Pilot projects enable managers to determine whether a system is appropriate for the organization's needs, has adequate capacity and flexibility, and is acceptable to employees.[6] Indeed, everyone gains experience in using the system. Management receives feedback from users and gains a general idea of the costs that will be incurred. This is particularly important in an organization where hard savings may be questionable, the extent of soft savings may be difficult to evaluate, and possible spin-off problems/benefits are unknown.

A pilot project gives managers time to experiment with and test a system, as well as to involve curious bystanders. It enables them to learn how to organize system activities, delegate work to subordinates, monitor procedures, and develop a format for reporting on use of the system. It also gives managers the chance to see exactly how much time they spend communicating and controlling information flow.

The pilot project should have a specific goal and well-defined parameters, such as reducing the turnaround time of an operation or increasing its output. It is not a good idea, however, to carry out long-term tasks or processes as a way of testing the equipment or a training program. When a simple project has been completed, a more complex activity can be attempted, as long as it can be divided into clearly defined, short-term segments.

The manager of office automation for the United Services Automobile Association (USAA) suggests that organizations establish tracking mechanisms if their equipment does not provide them. In this way, they can determine whether system software modifications need to be made.[7] In addition, he offers the following tips from his own company's experience:

- Keep typewriters. USAA had trouble using its system to complete certain preprinted forms.
- Do not be too ambitious with a training program. USAA had a 16-hour, full-featured training program where people learned "too much, too fast" and forgot what they learned. As a result, he suggests training people in specific areas, e.g., file management and scheduling events and locations.
- "Do not take support from other departments for granted."

As part of an EM pilot project, a Philadelphia company held a "paper-free" day to make personnel aware of their dependence on paper and alert them to the ways in which electronic mail could serve their communications needs.[8] Holding a reception at the beginning or end of the pilot project also makes people more aware of the system.

## BUILDING A FOUNDATION OF USERS

Initially, the new EM system should be promoted by outgoing, congenial people who will be willing to "talk it up" and share their experiences with others. Good-natured boosters are usually more influential in getting a system accepted and used than are people steeped in its technology. Management can also cultivate groups of people who have similar titles or who do related work and those who express general interest in communicating via EM. This effort can be supported by scheduling monthly receptions for "joiners."

Executives who have long-term EM experience stress the importance of starting a system with a large group of users who need to communicate daily. Such people will get involved more quickly and more often. Insufficient numbers of participants or insufficient use of a system can create start-up problems.

An important step in promoting an EM system can take place when individuals and groups are first interviewed about their work requirements and their preferences for particular communications systems and patterns. Interviewing time can also be used to solicit commitment to the organization's plans. Communications experts suggest that interviewers describe the electronic mail system as a new service that makes work easier, rather than as new hardware that people must learn about.

Interviewers may find that people who are unfamiliar with electronic mail will be uninterested or negative about using a new system. These individuals may require more extensive interviewing, and their comments should be analyzed. One consultant suggests simply ignoring negative responses.

Organizations with art departments should produce their own eye-catching posters and brochures. They should also promote the new EM system in company newsletters, on bulletin boards, and in local publications.

# TRAINING USERS

A vital part of implementing EM is setting up user training sessions. Where an organization has a training department, management should ask for its guidance in writing programs designed for specific tasks. Teaching segments are known to be most effective when they are brief and to the point. Incorporating graphics also helps to reinforce teaching.

Hands-on workshops can be used to simulate planned EM patterns, explain what makes a system tick, and show how it can be applied to the organization's communications/information-flow patterns. Training sessions should be relaxed, and participants should be encouraged to express their doubts and personal concerns about a system. Trainers should also be encouraged to discuss what the disadvantages or limitations of a system are, how to use back-up procedures if the system fails, and whom to call for help. Four or five sessions may be required before a user understands the benefits of a system and feels at ease with it.

Instruction guides, technical manuals, and sales brochures with different approaches are helpful during this phase of training. For complicated teleconferencing systems, video and audiocassettes, in addition to manufacturers' guidelines, can help steer users through the process.

Digital Equipment Corporation (DEC) developed both technical and nontechnical guides for its employees, as well as a plastic reference card summarizing EM commands. DEC also ran a hotline for people who encountered problems while using the system and created a feedback file into which suggestions and complaints could be sent while users were logged on. These were monitored daily.

In addition, the company gave personnel hands-on training sessions and provided additional training on request. Employees and management were pleased with the results, and personnel required little extra time for the learning procedure.[9]

# ENCOURAGING USER PARTICIPATION

Managers must consider the psychological aspects of introducing new equipment into the workplace. There are a number of attitudes and tactics in communicating that can be used to encourage the comfortable flow of ideas among participants and lessen the possibility of misunderstandings:

- Avoid bullying or verbally pushing participants.
- Provide feedback that informs users of the progress they are making and how their input is being received.
- Encourage passive participants to get involved by talking to them privately, via EM.
- Watch for an individual's electronic messaging style.

Those who manage an electronic mail or computer teleconferencing system must be responsive to users' technical questions and show respectful attention to users' concerns and reactions as they learn to relate to other employees in this new way.

Dr. Walter O. Roberts, the founder of the National Center for Atmospheric Research in Boulder, Colorado, suggests the following approach to using the system:

- Encourage people to practice, as in drivers' education.
- Develop a "buddy" system so that EM users will share ideas and support one another.
- Suggest ways of overcoming the fear of typing.
- Establish communication protocols—who speaks and when.
- Eliminate grammar and typography as issues.
- Establish discussions pertaining to the desired format.
- Send users news flashes or very short, one-sentence editorials, forceful opinions, or essays.

Managers can encourage user participation by personally endorsing a system and telling people that they use it and like the results. They can reinforce participation by using words like "good" or "fine" when well-written messages are received. These apparently insignificant measures go a long way toward creating favorable employee attitudes. Brief, animated, positive responses such as "I support that position!" are also effective when a manager receives a valuable, substantive message.

Specific tactics that help make a communications system more effective include the following:

- Vary the communication style, occasionally posing questions or asking for personal opinions.
- Place statements of more than one page in separate memos.
- Treat issues tactfully, being wary of "worst-interpretation" scenarios.
- Keep language simple, always defining terms, explaining remarks, and asking if more information is needed.
- Discuss personal experiences and common interests when relating to other individuals.

## THE PROBLEM OF "FLAMING"

When people use electronic mail systems, they have a tendency to communicate in an informal and terse manner. As a result, their messages are sometimes misunderstood, and "flaming" occurs. Flaming refers to the anger generated by ambiguous, terse, or thoughtless messaging. The hasty, critical responses that follow often lead to deep personal conflicts and grave managerial problems.

According to scientists at Carnegie-Mellon University, the root of the problem appears to be that electronic mail does not provide the same feedback that people get from in-person conversation. Visual cues that are a part of face-to-face interaction may, they propose, inhibit extreme behavior. Furthermore, they suspect that "using computers to communicate draws attention to the technology and to the content of communication and away from people and relationships with people."[10]

To avoid flaming, the Fort Collins, Colorado, Police Department has developed an informal EM code of behavior.[11] The head of the department suggests discussing the issue with all users and offers the following advice:

- Never send an electronic message when angry. Rather, set it aside and re-examine the contents later.
- If you think you have sent a potentially inflammatory message, follow it up immediately with an apology.
- If you receive a "flamer" followed by an apology, disre-

gard the flamer. Be gracious, because, over time, you may also send a flamer or two that you hope will be forgiven.

To promote attitudes of trust and optimism among its members, the police department has established a "praise network." This is used by employees to let each other know they have done a nice job and are appreciated.

## THE UNUSED SYSTEM

When electronic mail goes unused, corporate management is likely to believe it has opted for a system which is too advanced for the organization. The problem, however, is usually that the organization did not thoroughly study its communications and information-flow patterns before choosing the EM system, and personnel were not sufficiently trained or encouraged to use it. Thus, they never became comfortable with this way of messaging and clung to their old communications habits.

Naturally, people who have lost messages or information will tend to avoid using the system, as will those who depend on rapid communications and experience system degradation. Degradation is the slowing of transmission caused by any one of a number of problems, particularly system overload. Needless to say, this is a frustrating experience for those dependent on swift communicating.

A system's effectiveness will also be limited by the psychological characteristics of an office and its management. One manager said that until he found how EM could support his position, he believed it would force him to relinquish a degree of the personal power he experienced in face-to-face meetings. The following factors are usually at the heart of such limitations, however:[12]

- Management's failure to use EM. It is not unusual for supervisors to involve their secretaries in electronic messaging while keeping at arm's length from the keyboard themselves. When this is the case, more paperwork is generated, time is lost, and the possibility of error and misinterpretation is reintroduced into the procedure. (This picture is changing, however, as many managers are learning to type and to enjoy information control.)

- Managers' failure to use EM in situations where its speed, ease, economy, and flexibility would be particularly useful, such as when responses require lengthy, reflective answers, and work-in-progress or project reports must be forwarded periodically to superiors.
- The characteristic reluctance of managers to be *managed*, whether by existing or innovative communications systems.

Sometimes a system is too effective. At Westinghouse Electric Corporation, once employees grew accustomed to the electronic mail system, they became interested in using it for other purposes, such as reaching databases. When the service was not available, they felt they were "losing touch." Some managers were so enthusiastic about the system that they tended to expect subordinates to check their EM boxes during vacations and on weekends.[13]

# EVALUATING THE SYSTEM

When an organization has used an electronic messaging system for a reasonable period of time, management can survey the system's use and hold informal conversations with personnel to evaluate their attitudes towards it. Follow-up training sessions should be available at this time so that people who have become accustomed to the system can broaden their use of it. An organization making such an evaluation should remember, however, that electronic mail and computer teleconferencing facilitate new task schedules and operating methods. This, in turn, may force a change in management procedures.

When a new system has been in place for a while, organizations should also analyze the information/communications flow with an eye to its modification or redesign. Kelleher and Cross suggest that the following can extend the usefulness of an electronic communications system:[14]

- Instituting information management experiments.
- Encouraging users to design innovative applications for the system.
- Studying tasks to determine which communications procedures can be routinized. Examples might include distributing weekly EM newsletters and holding weekly audio conferences at which developments that affect a system or work procedure could be discussed.
- Encouraging creation of new internal/external networks.
- Taking a more flexible, creative approach to decision making by establishing electronic meetings.
- Selecting one project to illustrate a creative use of computer teleconferencing.

Managers can expand the use of a system by watching for possible new users and applications, checking for trends among users, and considering how technology can be added to the system. Terminals, systems, and working rooms can be modified according to users' needs. Other measures include advertising the EM system and writing up the users' experiences for internal company departments and for the local and trade press.

# 8 Measuring the Difference: How to Audit Communications and Evaluate EM Costs

## ANALYZING THE CURRENT PICTURE

An audit of current communications patterns requires detailed surveys of telephone, mail, internal memo, facsimile, and other communications systems. The audit should include the time and frequency of voice, data, and graphics transmissions as well as the length of messages (long legal drafts as opposed to short purchase order numbers, for example), the networks along which they travel, and their destinations. A study of organizational meetings and their associated travel costs is also necessary, particularly if computer teleconferencing is planned.

There are many sources for this information within a large corporation. A telecommunications staff, for example, is familiar with a company's existing electronic communications system(s) and knows whether a telephone-based messaging system would serve its needs. Data processing staff members know if interactive equipment that handles and stores information is appropriate for the company's messaging requirements. Office managers involved with automated equipment can contribute suggestions based upon their workstation experience.

In addition, managers can usually generate new viewpoints by talking with their counterparts in other companies, with vendors, and with telephone company representatives. It is some-

**157**

times necessary for an organization to hire a telecommunications specialist to develop a computerized model of a projected office system that will meet very specialized needs. Entirely new networking arrangements are occasionally necessary.

## How EM Can Reorganize and Reduce the Work Load

An organization can use the audit as a basis for reorganizing and eliminating some tasks. This involves (1) studying the communications patterns at individual and group levels, (2) learning the operating methods and objectives of each potential networking group, and (3) identifying the specific types of activity that EM would replace, i.e., telex, memos, telephone, or conferencing. Once these elements are identified, it will become clear how a new communications system might modify them.

As part of the auditing process and before introducing an electronic messaging system, it is important that employees be asked to track their telephone calls, including the purpose and duration of those calls. This allows them to see where electronic messaging will save them time and provide their company with more efficient, economical service than the telephone company can. Managers can use the opportunity to make it clear that electronic mail and voice messaging cost a fraction of the cost of telephone calls. In addition, employees will appreciate being brought into the evolving process.

The differences in cost and convenience when substituting electronic mail for telephone service are sometimes quite dramatic. The following example shows how Cities Service Company benefitted by using a global electronic messaging service.[1] An oil project engineer in Houston, a consulting engineer in Tulsa, and a drilling manager in Manila were holding telephone conferences each morning regarding drilling activities. By communicating asynchronously via computer, they conveniently bridged their 14-hour time zone differences and "eliminated over $100,000 worth of capital expenses that would have been incurred in Manila had the system not been installed."

The manager in Manila entered his reports into the communications network in the morning (Manila time). The Houston and Tulsa engineers took their portable computer terminals home and were able to check the Manila report before going to bed or the following morning. This allowed convenient, effective, around-the-clock discussion among the project participants.

## How EM Can Eliminate or Support Meetings

Organizations should re-evaluate the roles of their regular face-to-face meetings and analyze the goals of those meetings. Are they usually met? What kind of information is circulated? What audiovisual props are typically used? How effective are they? The organization can then determine if EM will substitute for, and thus provide a less costly alternative to, some face-to-face meetings.

Where in-person meetings must be held, EM is best used as a support system. It can serve as an organizer and a timesaver when used to background participants on upcoming discussion topics and to clarify thorny issues that must be discussed. EM can also facilitate and shorten face-to-face meetings when people use it as a forum to reconcile minor differences of opinion beforehand and eliminate the unnecessary and often petty side issues that arise during meetings. Experience has shown that problems requiring resolution by any two participants and potentially emotional issues can often be defused in this way.

There are several other ways in which managers can use EM to support regularly held meetings. For example, conferees can be provided with an electronic newsletter or bulletin board (files accessible to all conferees) into which they can enter information and ideas relevant to the conference agenda. Or a manager can prepare a proposed agenda and forward it to all prospective participants via EM, with agenda suggestions or changes allowed for a given period of time. Theoretically, even a meeting participant visiting a company facility abroad can be informed of proposed discussion topics on the organization's EM network.

# AUDITING USERS' ATTITUDES TOWARD AUTOMATION

To successfully implement an electronic mail system and eliminate potential "surprises," it is important not only to analyze communications patterns but also to study and understand users' attitudes toward automation. In a study designed to determine key workers' attitudes toward automation,[2] the consulting firm of Booz, Allen & Hamilton found that although these workers were interested in automation and wanted "to reshape their time profiles," they had some trepidation about the automation process and its ultimate usefulness.

The study showed that "less productive" activities (traveling, waiting for meetings to start, doing essentially clerical tasks, etc.) occupied 25 percent of the subjects' time, and that the use of more highly automated support systems could save them an average of 15 percent of their working time over five years. Despite this evidence that automated systems enhance productivity, the study found that "most decision makers are skeptical about what managerial work stations, personal computers [etc.] . . . can do for their businesses . . . and they lack confidence that their organizations can channel and measure the intended benefits." On a personal level, those questioned worried about how they would deal with these new electronic tools.

The study also indicated, however, that knowledge workers are more inclined to accept the idea of automation if it is introduced with a focus on reducing less-productive time—a frequently expressed source of dissatisfaction among those interviewed. Other ways suggested to counter the natural resistance to automation were to involve users early in the selection process and to make no demands that all workers must accept the system.

# EVALUATING EM COSTS

The costs of a proposed electronic mail system can be considered in terms of the "hard" and "soft" savings it will provide.

Hard savings are the measurable differences between a company's present costs and its projected costs once the new communications and information-handling systems are integrated. Hard savings include costs related to travel and office time lost while people are away at meetings. They also include cost differences between shipping material by courier and transmitting material via EM. Other examples of hard savings include the time/cost savings gained by being able to update inventories electronically, reach categories or lists of people quickly, and work cooperatively to produce reports.

Soft savings are generally difficult to measure directly. They are implied in statements like: "Electronic mail makes it easier to collaborate," "EM saves time," and "EM improves management productivity, office efficiency, and business opportunities."

Soft savings are usually produced by a complex string of activities of overriding importance to an operation. When a single element like time is saved, it is easy to see the source. But when a number of elements contribute to soft savings, it is more difficult to identify or evaluate each contribution. The following story illustrates the difficulty of measuring soft savings. In this case they include the value of the time saved by a publisher and his team of writers, the accuracy of transmissions provided, and the success of the publisher's enterprise.

A publisher of technical newsletters had the problem of getting reporters to deliver their stories to him "fast, but accurately." He used technical writers living throughout the country who supplied economic information and technical stories for the newsletters.

Because the publisher found that reporters' dictation of information and stories by telephone was imprecise, courier service costly, and the U.S. Postal Service inconvenient, he sent each reporter a facsimile (fax) machine to use in communicating with him. Although fax provides only station-to-station transmission of printed copy over telephone lines, the publisher was able to send story ideas, graphic materials, and feedback on his employees' writing, knowing they would receive it within minutes. The reporters, in turn, were assured that their articles and information would arrive when they were transmitted, and in time for publication.

# IN-HOUSE ELECTRONIC MAIL VERSUS TIME-SHARING SERVICES _____

Most personal computer owners and businesses that are not financially prepared to establish in-house networks use time-sharing facilities. These organizations typically own teletype-writers, PCs, data processing computers, or other communicating devices and need access to a computer that can control electronic messaging flow and other operations.

Organizations that must choose between using a time-sharing service and establishing an in-house electronic mail system should consider the following factors:

- Costs of new systems and their implementation.
- Current equipment—its utility and maintenance.
- Short-term versus long-term needs.
- Present and projected communications strategies for moving information to the right place at the right time. This would include office automation plans for the role of voice messaging and data transfer.
- Number of potential users, their locations, and the type and volume of their messages.
- Requirement for one-way or interactive service.
- Response time required when communicating.
- Network structures and line-control procedures that would be required for a potential EM system.

# ADVANTAGES OF TIME-SHARING _____

The primary advantage of time-sharing is that no capital investment in the purchase and maintenance of costly equipment is required. Second, using a time-sharing service gives an organization the opportunity to test a particular EM system while it determines actual EM communications needs and familiarizes its personnel with the electronic messaging concept.

Third, it is easy to operate. After subscribing to a time-sharing service, an individual or organization can reach the service computer by simply connecting the word processor, computer, or other communicating device to a modem and then dialing the appropriate number.

Fourth, the costs are reasonable. The costs of using time-sharing services vary widely and depend on the following factors:

- Number of messages sent.
- Telephone calling time. (Costs vary according to the time of day or night.)
- Character transmission and transmission speed.
- Connection costs.
- Rush-message surcharges.
- Electronic storage.
- Monthly subscription fee.
- Special report charges.
- Broadcast fees.
- Other special services.

Electronic messaging, calculated by the hour, costs about $15 per hour during working hours, less during off-peak periods. Currently, the average message costs between $.50 and $1.00.

Time-sharing services available include the following:

- Sourcemail℠, Source Telecomputing Corporation, McLean, Virginia, a subsidiary of Reader's Digest Association.
- Comet™ Electronic Mail System, Computer Corporation of America, Cambridge, Massachusetts.
- InfoMail™ Electronic Mail System, Bolt, Baranek and Newman, Cambridge, Massachusetts.
- GTE's Telemail℠.
- CompuServe™, Dayton, Ohio.

Major public data networks such as Uninet, Telenet, and Tymnet are joining with companies that specialize in electronic mail and are expected to provide more fully integrated, competitive, and comprehensively managed global EM service. This upgraded service will facilitate communication between individuals and organizations having equipment that runs at different speeds and uses different codes and protocols. EM providers that do not have their own network facilities must channel messaging through leased public or private communications networks.

## CHOOSING FROM AMONG TIME-SHARING SERVICES

The major factor in choosing an EM time-sharing service should be its ease of operation. It should also provide a range of managerial support features that go beyond the basic creating, sending, filing, and deleting of messages. There are significant differences in the way EM systems handle files, the length of material they will accept and transfer, and the choice of sending times they make available. Sophisticated systems provide adequate filing space and high-quality editing capability.

Quick messaging retrieval is important to people operating on tight schedules. It is therefore essential that a user be able to find messages through cross-referencing. This is done by keying in codes for sender, date sent, topic, and word or other category. It is also important that the user be able to sequence messages numerically. When a message has been lost in transmission, or an individual has simply failed to "mail" a promised electronic letter, numerical sequencing lets the sender determine its exact status.

The ability to set up distribution lists and send mail to an entire category or list of people is also a great timesaver, as is an on-line reference directory for addressing mail. Another handy EM managerial feature permits the user to create "alias" mailboxes. These let users automatically place messages in a special category or file them under a specific heading. Secretarial handling is thus eliminated. Electronic scheduling and calendaring features also reduce secretarial interaction and paper shuffle.

Security precautions should not be overlooked in considering an EM time-sharing system. With a growing number of users accessing communications networks, privacy of information has become a major concern. In the opinion of some researchers, it will continue to be a problem. Most time-sharing services protect their users by providing them with special identification numbers or code words for accessing a system. Some services require a second password to provide an extra measure of privacy. Yet even these procedures have proved to be an insufficient barrier against "computer criminals" (sometimes referred to as "hackers") who have cracked entry codes and gained access to sensitive government and industry data. In some instances, entry was gained because codes were relatively easy to break. In other cases, system subscribers gave codes to unauthorized individuals.

Users of a time-sharing system also encounter the problem of degradation, or the slowing of a system when many people use it simultaneously or for other reasons. When a system degrades, the user must wait longer to enter a message or receive a response. A prospective user can check on this problem before subscribing to a system by asking other subscribers for their experience with the particular system.

## SMALLER ELECTRONIC MAIL PROVIDERS

Many personal computer (PC) and communicating word processor (CWP) owners do not realize there are a number of smaller companies that can provide them with selected EM services. Depending on the individual's equipment and needs, these services can establish electronic mail connections with most communicating devices in the United States and abroad. Their computers convert incompatible terminal signals and will hold electronic messages until they are requested, or for a reasonable period of time.

For example, a PC or CWP owner (using a modem and telephone line) can communicate via EM with either a telex (50 baud) or TWX (110 baud) device by obtaining an account with Graphnet of Teaneck, New Jersey, or Speeditelex International of Atlanta. These services put the individual in touch with a large part of the 1.5 million teleprinters throughout the United States and the world.

For PC owners who have modems and want to communicate with people having similar equipment, the software program TLX-A-SYST™, of American International Communications, Boulder, Colorado, enables them to:

- Send and receive messages and cables through the I.T.T. Timetran℠ service.
- Print or display stored messages and a traffic log.
- Establish, view, or modify a personal directory.
- Store messages on disks for later display.

GRAM-A-SYST™, also of American International Communications, provides another EM software package that connects the user to Western Union's EasyLink℠ service. EasyLink℠ switching provides:

- Communication with U.S. and worldwide telex service.
- Connections to Mailgram, telegram, and cablegram service.
- Intra-company low-cost networks.
- PCs, CWPs, and portable computer terminals.
- Automatic answering facsimile equipment.

MIST™ and Mighty Mail™ are similar personal computer software systems offered by New Era Technologies of Washington, D.C. Mighty Mail™ operates at 1200-baud rates and is designed to automate the logging-on, commands, sending, and collection of mail. This fast processing substantially reduces total messaging costs.

## ESTABLISHING AN IN-HOUSE SYSTEM

An in-house EM system can be based on a network of devices linked via a local area network or a private branch exchange (PBX) system (a company's private internal telephone system), or by purchasing a complete and running electronic mail "turn-key" operation. It can also be based on a packaged software program that permits terminals to interface with a network service.

Once they are installed and maintained, in-house EM systems are very economical for large organizations. Some companies have brought costs down to about $.10 for an average domestic message and $.20 for a message sent abroad. In-house systems can usually be customized to meet an organization's specific needs. In the long run, customization proves to be a cost-saving approach. In-house equipment also provides better editing facilities for creating messages.

Much of the office equipment now available possesses communicating potential and will interact in an in-house system when bridged to a local area network (LAN), a private branch exchange (PBX) internal telephone system, or a time-sharing network. Where the existing office devices are not designed to interact, appropriate interfaces can usually overcome the problem.

# THE TELECOMMUTING ALTERNATIVE

Telecommuting is an alternative working arrangement appropriate for some employees. An article in *Forbes* magazine suggests that telecommuting can provide a successful work arrangement for intelligent, self-motivated, self-disciplined people who have personal computers or word processors and either prefer to or have to work at home. The advantages of the arrangement quickly become disadvantages, however, if the home situation includes demanding children or pets, frequent telephone interruptions, and responsibility for household chores.[3]

Before considering a telecommuting program, an organization should measure the existing patterns of communication and make a financial analysis of the work being performed. The next step is to assess the hardware and software necessary to accomplish both present and future telecommuting work, and any problems of security that might arise in handling the prospective job. Likewise, additional equipment, furniture, safety, and care for the "office away from the office" must be considered.

The organization considering telecommuting must keep a number of issues clearly in mind.[4] For example, the first project should be considered a pilot project. Any proposed short- or long-term work should have a clearly defined structure so that it can be easily implemented and evaluated. Both the employer's and the employee's responsibilities regarding project scheduling and segmentation should also be thoroughly discussed and agreed upon. Likewise, the conditions under which the work is carried out should be clarified. If telecommuting means that the employee will be out of the manager's sight and possibly out-of-mind as well, the effect of telecommuting on the employee's career path should be discussed.

A 1981 Diebold study suggested that telecommuting jobs require:[5]

- A minimal amount of equipment and space.
- Little face-to-face contact with other people—and when communication is required, it can be easily handled by telephone or "batched" during the time the employee is in the office.
- Concentration and large blocks of time when the employee works independently of others.
- Project orientation, each project resulting in defined deliverables.
- Projects that can be completed with minimum-term deadlines (approximately two weeks to four months).
- Little close supervision, and working conditions that are not subject to union scrutiny.

Other studies, however, indicate that for effective work-at-home projects, a surprising amount of equipment and space is necessary, and a special working relationship between managers and telecommuters is required. In one instance, an oil company analyst required the following equipment for telecommuting:

- Personal computer
- Hard-disk drive
- Printer
- Monitor
- Modem
- Telecopier (facsimile)
- Special room or home office
- Desk and chair
- Filing cabinet
- Typewriter
- Lighting fixtures

The employer and employee established the following work-at-home relationship:

- Daily psychological support from supervisor.
- Weekly trips to the office for meeting and mail pickup.
- Weekly project reviews.
- Scheduled reports for a history of effectiveness.

Although people in various walks of life have accommodated themselves well to telecommuting and prefer it as a way of working, both physical and psychological problems can face the electronic home workplace—particularly when independent telecommuters (entrepreneurs) contract for work. Equipment does not always function, and material that has not been "backed up" may simply disappear. When home operators buy devices piecemeal from different vendors, they sometimes neglect to purchase adequate service contracts.

In reviewing surveys on telecommuting, *Forbes* writers found the following trends:[6]

- People will be telecommuting part-time or for half-year periods rather than working full-time or for lifetime careers.
- Middle- and upper-management employees may feel insecure working outside the corporate picture. They also feel more confident in face-to-face decision making.
- Most people crave peer approval and are more comfortable working in a group setting.

The *Forbes* review also quotes organizations such as the 9 to 5 National Association of Working Women and unions as expressing concern that this information-age cottage industry provides the opportunity for worker exploitation and "should be banned."

# PREPARING FOR EQUIPMENT PURCHASE OR LEASE

Electronic mail system costs can be categorized in three ways, according to (1) transmission costs, (2) terminal, computer, and software costs, and (3) maintenance costs.

To prepare an economic evaluation of a proposed electronic mail system and its installation, management should first describe the existing communications system, accounting for:

- Its degree of obsolescence.
- Compatibility of equipment.
- Service and support costs.
- Training requirements.
- Back-up and alternatives.
- Auditing criteria.
- Management and organizational impact.

This should be followed by an introduction to the proposed system and a financial analysis summary that covers capital expenses for the system and the required implementation methods, as well as the recurring and displaced costs.

# Resource Guide

## Commercial Electronic Mail Packages and Systems

COMET™
Computer Corp. of America
675 Massachusetts Ave.
Cambridge, MA 02139

CROSS/POINT™
Cross Information Co.
1881 9th, Suite 311
Boulder, CO 80302-5151

EASYLINK℠
Western Union
One Lake St.
Upper Saddle River, NJ 07458

INFOMAIL™
BBN Computer Corp.
33 Moulton St.
Cambridge, MA 02238

INFONET℠
Infonet Computer Sciences Corp.
718 17th St., Suite 500
Denver, CO 80202

INFOPLEX℠
CompuServe, Inc.
5000 Arlington Centre Blvd.
Columbus, OH 43220

MCI MAIL℠
MCI
2000 M St., N.W.
Washington, DC 20036

ONTYME℠
Tymshare, Inc.
20705 Valley Green Dr.
Cupertino, CA 95014

TELEMAIL℠
GTE Telenet, Inc.
8229 Boone Blvd.
Vienna, VA 22180

SOURCEMAIL℠
Source Telecomputing Corp.
1616 Anderson Rd.
McLean, VA 22102

ZAPMAIL℠
Federal Express
Local Federal Express address

ADP
405 Rte. 3
Clifton, NJ 07015

Advanced Micro Techniques
1291 E. Hillsdale Blvd., #209
Foster City, CA 94404

Applied Data Research (283)
Rte. 206 & Orchard Rd.
Princeton, NJ 08540

Applied Data Systems, Inc.
P.O. Box 5090
Scottsdale, AZ 85261

AT&T-Communications
Rte. 202/206
Bedminster, NJ 07921

**171**

AT&T Information Systems
P.O. Box 6835
Bridgewater, NJ 08807

CASCORP/Computer Associated
   Services Corp.
P.O. Box 504
Arlington Heights, IL 60006

Cawthon Scientific Group
24224 Michigan Ave.
Dearborn, MI 48124

CMS, Inc.
846 N. 6th St.
San Jose, CA 95112

Computer Associates Intl.
125 Jericho Turnpike
Jericho, NY 11753

Devcom Mid America, Inc.
2603 W. 22nd St.
Oakbrook Terrace, IL 60181

High Technology Software, Inc.
P.O. Box 60406
1611 N.W. 23rd
Oklahoma City, OK 73146

Information Management
   Consultants & Assoc., Inc.
P.O. Box 5963
Metairie, LA 70009

International Electronic Mail
   Service (IEMS)
21686 Steven Creek
Cupertino, CA 94105

ITT Dialcom, Inc.
1109 Spring St.
Silver Spring, MD 20910

Lotus Development Corp.
161 First St.
Cambridge, MA 02138

Microcom
1400A Providence Hwy.
Norwood, MA 02062

Microstuf
1845 The Exchange, #205
Atlanta, GA 30339

NEC America, Inc.
2740 Prosperity Ave.
Fairfax, VA 22031

Northern Telecom
111311 Winners Circle Dr.
Los Alamitos, CA 90720

Orion Software, Inc.
400-2 Totten Pond Rd., #200
Waltham, MA 02154

Philadelphia Consulting Group
P.O. Box 102
Wynnewood, PA 19096

Pro Computing
One Penn Plaza, #3314
New York, NY 10119

Rapicom
3001 Orchard Pkwy.
San Jose, CA 94134

Satellite Business Systems
8283 Greensboro Dr.
McLean, VA 22102

I. P. Sharp Assoc., Inc.
2 First Canadian Pl., #1900
Toronto, ON
Canada M5X 1E3

Software Connections
1800 Wyatt Dr., #17
Santa Clara, CA 95054

Software Marketing Group
160 13th St.
Olathe, KS 66062

Sydney Development Corp.
600-1385 W. 8th Ave.
Vancouver, BC
Canada V6H 3V9

Telephone Software Connection,
Inc.
P.O. Box 6548
Torrance, CA 90504

Transend Corp.
2190 Paragon Dr.
San Jose, CA 94536

Unicomp Corp.
202 Plaza Towers
Springfield, MO 65804

## Consulting & Training

Cross Information Co.
1881 9th, Suite 311
Boulder, CO 80302-5151

Virginia A. Ostendorf, Inc.
P.O. Box 2896
Littleton, CO 80161

## Industry Association

Electronic Mail Association
1919 Pennsylvania Ave., N.W.,
Suite 300
Washington, DC 20006

# Notes

## Chapter 1

1. Ernest C. Baynard and Anne A. Armstrong, "Electronic Mail Gets Through at White House, U.S.D.A." ("Washington Wrap-up" column), *Management Technology*, November 1983, p. 59.
2. Virginia Inman, "MCI Mail, Falling Short of Expectations, Begins Campaign to Increase Service's Use," *Wall Street Journal*, March 16, 1984, sec. 2, p. 25.
3. William F. Buckley, Jr., "A Practical Use for Computer" (Universal Press Syndicate column), *Daily Camera* (Boulder, CO), January 18, 1984, p. 12.
4. *New York Times*, October 10, 1983, sec. 4, p. 1, col. 4.
5. Interview with Pat Kelly, Division Director, Police Department, Fort Collins, CO, August 30, 1984.
6. Erik Eckholm, "Emotional Outbursts Punctuate Conversations by Computer," *New York Times*, October 2, 1984, p. 19.
7. Doug Brooks, "The One Percent Solution," *Government Computer News*, March 1984, p. 75.
8. H. Edward Nyce and Richard Groppa, "Electronic Mail at MHT" (information from chart), *Management Technology*, May 1983, p. 71.
9. "Hidden Hurdles of Expanding a Pilot System," *EM World* (newsletter, Silver Spring, MD), March 12, 1984, p. 4.
10. PACTEL, Subsidiary of PA International Consulting Group, London, England, 1983.
11. Eckholm, op. cit.
12. John M. Williams and John Collins III, "Federal Electronic Mail Usage Spreading," *Government Computer News*, September 1983, p. 22.
13. John Lusa, "Editor's Notes," *Telecommunication Products + Technology*, March 1984, p. 3.
14. Kevin Strelho, "Mail Call, Mail Call!," *Personal Computing*, December 1983, p. 126.
15. Henry Nothhaft, "Making a Case for Using Electronic Mail," *Data Communications*, May 1982, p. 85.
16. "Michigan Lawmaker 'Talks' to Constituency via Computer" (Associated Press), *Daily Camera* (Boulder, CO), January 25, 1984, p. 12A.

17. Kathy Bissell, "Inauguration of Electronic Mail Aids Congressman," *Communications News*, September 1982, p. 90C.
18. Baynard and Armstrong, op. cit.
19. Nothhaft, op. cit.
20. Desmond Smith, "The Wiring of Wall St.," *New York Times Magazine*, October 23, 1983, p. 44 f.
21. "Shifting Personal Computer Market" (information from chart; source: Future Computing, Inc.), *New York Times*, September 16, 1983, p. D1.
22. *Sourceworld* (newsletter published by The Source™, McLean, VA), February 1984, pp. 1, 3.
23. Kathleen Wiegner and Ellen Paris, "A Job with a View," *Forbes*, September 12, 1983, pp. 143-150.
24. "Summer Olympics to Be Linked by Electronic Messaging System," *Communications News*, November 1983, p. 98.

**Chapter 2**

1. Daniel Bell, "A Revolution at Electronic Speed," *For Members Only* (American Express brochure), Fall 1983, p. 3.
2. Ibid.
3. Ronald A. Frank, "On the Way to Oz: Bumps in the Yellow Brick Road" ("Focus/Teleprocessing" column), *Business Communications Review*, September/October 1980, p. 3.
4. C. A. Ross, "Compatibility—The Key to Office Automation," 11th Annual *Interface '83 Proceedings* (New York: McGraw-Hill, 1983), p. 173.
5. Jean Tally, "Medicine by Machine," *Graduating Engineer Computing Careers*, October 1983, p. 50.
6. William Gates, "The Future of Software Design," *Byte*, August 1983, p. 401.
7. Andrew Pollack, "Japan's Push in Fiber Optics," *New York Times*, July 30, 1984, sec. 4, p. 1.

**Chapter 3**

1. Charles H. Divine, "Office Automation: Facing the Challenge," 11th Annual *Interface '83 Proceedings* (New York: McGraw-Hill, 1983), pp. 192-197.
2. "Reliability, Not Price, Seen First Priority in OA Equipment," *Computerworld*, October 24, 1983, p. 81.
3. Jeffrey R. Duerr, Garn Nelson, and Christene Wade, "Modems: Features and Functions—Part 8 in a Series," *Telephony*, November 10, 1980, p. 69.

## Chapter 4

1. W. A. Saxton and Morris Edwards, "Which Route for Electronic Mail?" ("Datacomm Directions" column), *Infosystems*, December 1980, p. 80.
2. H. Edward Nyce and Richard Groppa, "Electronic Mail at MHT," *Management Technology*, May 1983, pp. 65-72.
3. John M. McQuillan, "Why Go to Electronic Mail?," *Computerworld*, September 28, 1981, pp. 9-10.
4. Jacques Vallee, *Computer Message Systems* (New York: Data Communications–McGraw-Hill, 1984), pp. 39-48.
5. "Bank Streamlines Communications with Mail System," *Computerworld*, September 12, 1983, pp. 147-148.
6. Nyce and Groppa, op. cit.
7. "Shifting Personal Computer Market" (information from chart; source: Future Computing, Inc.), *New York Times*, September 16, 1983, p. D1.
8. David Ferris, "The Micro-Mainframe Connection," *Datamation*, November 1983, p. 126.
9. Michael Tyler, "Portable Computer: How High Can It Fly?," *Datamation's Dataguide*, 1983, p. 182.
10. John Seaman, "Voicemail: Should Computers Carry Your Mail?," *Computer Decisions*, November 1983, p. 189.
11. "Voice Messaging System Improves Productivity of Marketing Staff," *Communications News*, June 1983, p. 46.
12. Ray Leffler, "Evaluating Needs for Integrating Voice and Data," *The Office*, August 1983, p. 86.
13. Interview with Bruce Thiemens, Peter Pan Seafood, Inc., Seattle, WA, December 20, 1984.
14. Sam Fedida and Rex Malik, *The Viewdata Revolution* (New York: John Wiley & Sons, 1979), pp. 50-63.
15. John M. Williams, "Postal Governors Order E-COM Sold," *Government Computer News*, July 1984, p. 4.
16. Stephen J. Shaw, "Heard on the Hill," *Mini-Micro Systems*, April 1984, p. 59.
17. Jim Seymour, "Electronic Mail: OA's Sleeping Giant Awakens," *Today's Office*, January 1984, p. 24.
18. "New Dispute on Postal Service's Electronic Mail," *New York Times*, June 16, 1984, p. 17.
19. *Electronic Mail Association*, vol. 1, no. 1, Spring-Summer 1984, p. 2.
20. Norman Black, "Electronic Mail Use Grows" (Associated Press), *Daily Camera* (Boulder, CO), August 21, 1984, p. 10.

### Chapter 5

1. "Market Views," *Systems and Software*, March 1983, p. 3.
2. Wayne Hall and George Salser, "Automating the Office Means Implementing the Network!," *Telecommunications Products + Technology*, March 1984, p. 6.
3. Ibid.
4. David E. Sanger, "Wiring M.I.T. for Computers," *New York Times*, February 17, 1984, p. 31.
5. Amtel Systems information on Messenger II™, Sunnyvale, CA.

### Chapter 6

1. Figures derived from data collected by James Bair of Bell Northern Research; Bolt, Baranek and Newman, Inc., Cambridge, MA, 1980 report "Electronic Mail: The Messaging System Approach"; Booz, Allen & Hamilton figures of Gerald Tellesen; IBM/SRI data of A. Martin, 1979; and *Technology Management*, State of the Art Report, ser. 10, no. 8, Pergamon Infotech, by B. Hubbard.
2. Interview with Bill Spencer, computer technologist with New Era Technologies, Washington, DC, September 1, 1984.
3. Kathleen Kelleher and Thomas Cross, *Tele/Conferencing: Linking People Together* (Englewood Cliffs, NJ: Prentice-Hall, 1985), p. 59.
4. Murray Turoff and Starr Roxanne Hiltz, "Computer Support for Group Versus Individual Decisions," *Special Issue on Communications in the Automated Office* (submitted to IEEE Transactions on Communications), July 1981, p. 4.
5. Steve Lohr, "The Japanese Challenge," *New York Times Magazine*, July 8, 1984, p. 41.
6. Bernard Husbands, "Electronic Mail—Applications for Management," *Journal of Systems Management*, August 1982, p. 8.
7. Andrew S. Grove, "How (and Why) to Run a Meeting," *Fortune*, July 11, 1983, pp. 134-135.
8. Conference on the bioconversion of lignocellulosics to fuel, fodder, and food held May-December 1983 to focus on processes and products suitable for developing countries. Designed to assess computer conferencing in communicating among participants in this type of field.

### Chapter 7

1. John Lusa, "Editor's Notes," *Telecommunication Products + Technology*, March 1984, p. 3.
2. Scott C. Kerr, "Electronic Mail Enhances Productivity," *The Office*, August 1983, p. 144.

3. Jim Seymour, "OA's Sleeping Giant Awakens," *Today's Office*, January 1984, p. 29.
4. Cross Information Co., Boulder, CO, 1984.
5. Telemedia International, Denver, CO; Public Service Satellite Consortium, Washington, DC; Satellite Business Systems, McLean, VA; Picturephone Meeting Service, Bedminster, NJ.
6. *The Report on Electronic Mail* (Cambridge, MA: The Yankee Group, November 1979), pp. 30-36.
7. "Hidden Hurdles of Expanding a Pilot EM System," *EM World* (newsletter, Silver Spring, MD), March 12, 1984, p. 3.
8. Bob Stoffels, "Management Notes" column, *Telephone Engineer and Management*, September 15, 1980, p. 14.
9. *Innovators in Market Structuring* (Cambridge, MA: The Yankee Group, April/July 1978), sec. 12, p. 21.
10. Erik Eckholm, "Emotional Outbursts Punctuate Conversations by Computer," *New York Times*, October 2, 1984, p. 19.
11. Interview with Pat Kelly, Division Director, Police Department, Fort Collins, CO, August 30, 1984.
12. From interview with Kathleen Kelleher, teleconferencing specialist, on June 25, 1984.
13. Kerr, op. cit.
14. Kathleen Kelleher and Thomas Cross, *Tele/Conferencing: Linking People Together* (Englewood Cliffs, NJ: Prentice-Hall, 1985).

## Chapter 8

1. J. Stephen Costello, "Are You Ready to Automate Your Office?," 11th Annual *Interface '83 Proceedings* (New York: McGraw-Hill, 1983), pp. 161-170.
2. Harvey Poppel, "Who Needs the Office of the Future?," *Harvard Business Review*, November-December 1982, pp. 146-155. Copyright © 1982 by the President and Fellows of Harvard College; all rights reserved.
3. Kathleen Wiegner and Ellen Paris, "A Job with a View," *Forbes*, September 12, 1983, pp. 143-150.
4. Gerardine DeSanctis, "A Telecommuting Primer," *Datamation*, October 1983, pp. 214-220.
5. Ibid.
6. Wiegner and Paris, op. cit.
7. *Electronic Message Systems: The Technological Market and Regulatory Prospects*, report submitted to the Federal Communications Commission by Kalba Bowen Assoc., Inc., and the Center for Policy Alternatives, M.I.T., in fulfillment of FCC contract number 0236, 1978, p. 129.

# Glossary

**Abbreviated Addressing**. Using a short code to send a message to a pre-programmed address.

**Access**. To key into a system so that storing or retrieving information is possible.

**Access Time**. The interval between the time that information is called from storage to the time delivery is completed.

**Account Number**. A number that identifies a budget/billing unit and associated storage areas.

**Acoustic Coupler**. A modem that cradles a telephone handset during transmission. A microphone in the modem picks up telephone tones and translates them into digital signals that can be understood by the receiving computer. Conversely, a modem translates digital signals from a computer into audible tones that are transmitted over telephone lines.

**Action-Item List**. A list that contains reminders that are brought to a member's notice periodically or on a specific date.

**Active Terminals**. Terminals that are prepared to interact with other equipment and receive information.

**Alphanumeric**. Consisting of letters, numbers, and/or special characters.

**Analog Signal**. A continuous signal that varies in direct proportion to the strength of an input signal. Telephones transmit the human voice by converting sound waves into electrical analog signals.

**ANSI**. American National Standards Institute, a group whose codes and standards apply to the computer industry.

**Answer/Auto-Answer**. A modem function whereby the equipment senses an incoming ring signal on the telephone line and automatically connects the modem to the line.

**Application**. A specific program or task. Sorting employee records, which a computer can execute, would be an example.

**Application Program**. A computer program designed to meet specific user needs, such as controlling inventory or monitoring a manufacturing process.

**Applications Software**. Same as application program.

**Architecture.** The design or organization of a system. Computer architecture refers to the central processing unit.

**Archive.** A record of information. Messages are stored on archive disks.

**Arithmetic Capability.** Ability of the system to perform calculating functions, such as addition, subtraction, multiplication, and division.

**Array.** Data in a row or matrix arrangement.

**Artificial Intelligence (AI).** Computer programming that recognizes ideas and answers problems. A system may have sensory perception. AI is used in robotics and "expert systems" where there is a base of specialized knowledge and a program from which a computer can solve problems.

**ASCII (American Standard Code for Information Interchange) Code.** A binary number assigned to each alphanumeric character and several non-printing characters that are used to control printers and communication devices.

**Assembly Language.** A programming language based on a computer's structure and machine language.

**Assistant.** An assistant in a computer conference group or center who is responsible for managing the public/private resources within his/her scope. Assistants are prohibited access to the content of items stored in private files. They serve as advisors within their organizational units.

**Asynchronous.** Not synchronized to work together. Asynchronous transmissions can be sent or received when participants choose, as opposed to being sent at fixed intervals.

**Attention Stack.** A storage facility for unfinished material (notes, messages, documents) that preserves its status while the user works on something else.

**Audio.** Voice portion of a communications link.

**Audio Conferencing.** Holding a telephone conference.

**Auto-Answer.** A feature that allows equipment to automatically receive and store information or messages until the recipient requests them.

**Autodial.** A modem function that enables a modem to dial telephone numbers.

**Automatic Carriage Return.** A system that automatically performs a carriage return. This permits the operator to continue typing without pausing at the end of each line.

**Automatic Pagination.** Division of a multipage document into pages having a specified new number of lines per page.

**Automatic Polling.** A system whereby one computerized device automatically requests another device to transmit information. Operators can specify times for equipment to "make calls," and send and collect messages.

**Automatic Sorting and Listing**. Sorting of items in numerical or alphabetical sequence or topic by which the file can be organized.

**Background**. Noninteractive services running on a computer while a person is using an interactive service.

**Background Processing**. The execution of a low-priority computer program when higher-priority programs are not using the system's sources.

**Back-up**. Copies of one or more files kept on a storage medium for insurance against loss.

**Bandwidth**. The range between the highest and lowest frequencies that a transmission channel can carry. A standard telephone line generally carries frequencies between 300 and 3,000 hertz (cycles per second), providing a bandwidth of 2,700 hertz.

**Baseband Transmission System**. A means of transmitting data on a local area network using coaxial cable or twisted-pair wire, digital signals, transceivers, and distributed control.

**BASIC (Beginners' All-purpose Symbolic Instruction Code)**. A widely used interactive programming language that is especially well suited to personal computers and beginning users.

**Batch Processing**. A technique of executing a set of computer programs without human interaction or direction. Under certain conditions direct interaction is possible.

**Baud**. A unit for measuring data transmission rates. Technically, baud rates refer to the number of times the communications line changes state after each second.

**Bell 103**. A protocol standard developed by Bell Telephone for modem communication at speeds below 300 baud.

**Bell 202**. A protocol used by modems for half-duplex transmission at speeds of up to 1200 baud.

**Bell 212**. A protocol used by modems for full-duplex transmission at speeds of up to 1200 baud.

**Bidirectional**. (1) Having the ability to transfer data in either direction. This is characteristic of a "bus" local area network. (2) Having the ability to print from right to left and from left to right. This increases the speed of a printing head.

**Binary**. Designating the fundamental number system used with computers. Binary numbers are represented by only two numerals, 0 and 1. The binary system is necessary because electrical circuits store and sense only two states: ON and OFF.

**BISYNC (BInary SYNChronous Communication)**. A method of transmission normally used by IBM mainframes. BISYNC gathers together a number of message characters and puts them in a single large message block that includes special characters, synchronized bits, and station addressing information.

**Bisynchronous**. Binary and synchronous signaling.

**Bit (Binary digIT)**. A unit of information that designates one of two possible values. A bit is usually written as a 1 or a 0 to represent the ON or OFF status of an electrical switch.

**Bit-Map Graphics**. A technology that allows control of individual pixels on a display screen and that produces graphic images of superior resolution. It permits accurate reproduction of arcs, circles, sine waves, or other curved images that block-addressing technology cannot accurately display.

**Black Box**. A device that connects incompatible hardware or software so that it can interact.

**Board**. Also "circuit board." A plastic resin board containing electronic components such as chips and the electronic circuits needed to connect them. *See also* Option Module.

**Boot**. To start up a system or program. A cold boot means a first start.

**BPS**. Bits per second.

**Bridge**. An electronic "place" where three or more people can confer by telephone, or in some cases by data terminal.

**Broadband Bus Network**. A coaxial cable network that is divided into a number of high-capacity channels able to carry data traffic, video, and voice transmissions. Many bits per unit of time can be moved from point to point.

**Broadband Channel**. A communications channel with a large bandwidth or capacity. Channels wider than voice grade are often considered to be broadband.

**Broadcasting**. Sending the same message to a number of people at the same time, from point-to-multipoint.

**Bubble Memory**. A type of memory composed of small magnetic domains formed on a thin crystal film of synthetic garnet. This system operates rapidly and holds informational content when power is turned off.

**Buffer**. A temporary memory storage area that holds information until equipment is able to process it. A buffer also holds data being passed between computers or other devices such as printers which operate at different speeds or different times.

**Bug**. Error in hardware or software programming.

**Bulletin Board**. An electronic file within an electronic mail or teleconferencing system. All participants can place or access public messages placed there.

**Bus**. A group of parallel electrical connections that carry signals between computer components or devices within a local area network.

**Byte**. The number of bits used to represent a character. For personal computers, a byte is usually eight bits.

**Cable**. A group of conductive elements, such as metal wires or fiber optic cable, packaged as a single line to interconnect communications systems.

**Cable Television**. A telecommunication system that uses coaxial cable to distribute the TV signal.

**CAI**. Computer-aided instruction.

**Calendar**. A permanent storage area associated with a group. It contains information about appointments, business trips, meetings, vacation times, etc., for each member of a conference group.

**Carrier**. A company that provides transmission capabilities for the general public.

**Cathode Ray Tube (CRT)**. A vacuum tube that generates and guides electrons onto a fluorescent screen to produce characters or graphic displays.

**CATV (Community Antenna Television System)**. Coaxial cable system that transmits television or other signals to subscribers from a single head-end location.

**CBMS (Computer-Based Message System)**. A sophisticated computer system that receives, stores, and transmits messages. Messages are delivered to the electronic mailboxes assigned to each user.

**CCITT**. Consultative Committee for International Telephony and Telegraphy, a part of the International Telecommunications Union that sets communications standards for the industry.

**Center**. A teleconference unit consisting of several members who have common interests or tasks. Members are provided with certain facilities like an electronic portfolio, bulletin board, and calendar to support their cooperative effort. A center manager establishes new centers, enrolls new members, and assigns roles to members, e.g., group manager or center assistant.

**Central Processing Unit (CPU)**. Electronic components that cause work in a computer to occur by interpreting instructions, performing calculations, moving data in main computer storage, and controlling the input/output operations. A CPU consists of the arithmetic/logic unit and the control unit.

**Channel**. A band of frequencies allocated for communications.

**Character**. A single printable letter (A-Z), numeral (0-9), or symbol (,%$.) used to represent data.

**Character Code**. Numerical values assigned to characters. The ASCII code is an example.

**Character Printer**. Equipment that prints one character at a time like a typewriter.

**Character Set**. The characters of a code, font, or device that can be generated and displayed.

**Chip**. Semiconductor material containing microscopic integrated circuits.

**Circuit**. (1) A system of semiconductors and related elements through which electrical current flows. (2) In data communications, the electrical path providing one-way or two-way communication between two points.

**Circuit Switching**. The physical connection taking place between channels.

**Coaxial Cable**. Cable that has one insulated conducting wire at the center. A second wire surrounds the insulation and is also insulated. Coaxial cable supports large bandwidth and has high data rates, high immunity to electrical interference, and low incidence of error.

**COBOL (COmmon Business-Oriented Language)**. A high-level programming language that is well suited to business applications involving complex data records (such as personnel files or customer accounts) and large amounts of printed output.

**CODEC (COder/DECoder)**. A chip in a telephone that converts an analog signal to a digital pulse, or the reverse.

**COM (Computer Output Microfilm Equipment)**. Devices used to record computer output as very small images on a roll or sheet of film.

**Command**. A user's instruction to the computer, generally given through a keyboard. This can be a word, mnemonic, or character that causes a computer to perform an operation.

**Communicating Word Processor**. A word processor that has been equipped to send and receive messages.

**Communication Capability**. The ability to transfer information between systems on and off premises.

**Communications Interface**. A system for converting keyboard signals to signals a network will accept.

**Communications Protocol**. *See* Protocol.

**Communications Satellite**. A satellite used to receive and retransmit data, video, and audio signals.

**Compatibility**. (1) The potential of an instruction, program, or component to be used on more than one computer. (2) The ability of computers to interact with other computers that are not necessarily similar in design or capabilities.

**Compiler**. A translator that renders a program in an computer's own machine language.

**Computer**. A programmable machine made up of a microprocessor, memory, keyboard, and monitor, which operate as a unit when instructions and power are applied.

**Computer Architecture**. Internal computer design based on the types of programs that will run on it and the number that can be run at one time.

**Computer Network**. An interconnection of computer systems, terminals, and communications facilities.

**Computer Program**. Instructions that tell a computer to do a specific task.

**Computer Teleconferencing**. Interactive group communication in which a computer is used to receive, hold, and distribute messages between participants for many-to-many communication.

**Concentrator**. A device that joins several communication channels.

**Configuration**. The arrangement of equipment (disks, diskettes, terminals, printers, etc.) in a particular system.

**Core Memory**. An early type of computer memory utilizing ferrite rings that represent binary data when the cores are magnetized in a particular direction. The integrated circuits used instead of cores in most modern computers are faster and smaller.

**CPU**. Central processing unit.

**Cross-Training**. Training employees in each other's duties.

**CRT**. *See* Cathode Ray Tube.

**CSMA/CD (Carrier Sense Multiple Access with Collision Detection)**. A system by which equipment on a LAN seeks to transmit a message. When it senses the network is idle, it will send information.

**Cursor**. A movable, blinking marker—usually a box or a line—on the terminal video screen that indicates the next point of character entry or change.

**Cursor Position**. The place where a specific function should be performed. "Home" is the upper left corner, and "reverse home" is the lower right corner.

**Daisy Wheel Printer**. A printer having characters on the ends of spokes that radiate from a plastic or metal wheel. As the wheel spins across the page, a hammer hits the appropriate characters, pressing them against the ribbon and onto paper.

**Data**. Facts, numbers, letters, and symbols that can be stored in a computer. For personal computer users, data can be thought of as the basic elements of information created or processed by an application program.

**Data Bank**. A collection of data which is stored on auxiliary storage devices.

**Database**. A large electronic collection of organized data that is required for performing a task. Typical examples are personnel files or stock quotations.

**Database Management Software**. A system of integrated tools to store, retrieve, and maintain a large collection of data. Some of the tools support functions like batch reporting, interactive query, and decision support.

**Database Management System**. A series of programs used to establish, update, and query a set of facts, figures, or any other information, e.g., an airline reservation system.

**Data Code**. A binary representation of a letter or number used by particular equipment.

**Data Communications**. Data transmission from one location to another using communications channels such as telephone lines, coaxial cables, microwaves, or other means.

**Data Diskette**. A diskette that is used entirely or primarily to contain data files.

**Data Processing**. The application in which a computer works primarily with numerical data, as opposed to text. Many computers can perform both data and text processing.

**Data Set**. (1) Another name for a modem. (2) A group of data elements.

**Decentralized Processing**. An arrangement whereby computers at remote locations communicate with a central processing unit but not directly with each other.

**Dedicated Computer**. A computer used for one special function, such as controlling the Space Shuttle's navigation system.

**Degradation**. Slowing of a data transmission as more users access a computer network, or for other reasons.

**Delete Capability**. The method(s) a system uses to delete information. It takes place by removing a document, page, paragraph, word, or character string.

**Device**. Hardware that performs a specific function or functions. Input devices (e.g., keyboard) are used to enter data into the CPU. Output devices (e.g., printer or display monitor) are used to take data out of a computer in some usable form. Input/output devices (e.g., terminal or disk drive) are able to perform both activities.

**Diagnostic Program.** A program that checks the operation of a device, board, or other component for malfunctions and errors, and reports its findings.

**Digital Signal.** A series of electrical impulses that carry information in computer circuits.

**Digitize.** To translate voice or pictorial signals into binary code (digital format) for transmission.

**Direct Connect Modem.** A modem that plugs directly into a telephone outlet, bypassing the handset. It enables users to send and receive signals directly to and from telephone lines. *See also* Acoustic Coupler.

**Direct Distance Dialing (DDD).** Accessing telephones tied to the public switched network by using the area code.

**Direct Memory Access (DMA).** A method for transferring data to or from a computer's memory without CPU intervention.

**Directory.** An index used by a control program to locate blocks of data that are stored in separate areas of a data set in direct access storage.

**Disk.** A flat, circular plate with a magnetic coating for storing data. Physical size and storage capacity of disks can vary. There are hard disks, diskettes (also called floppy disks), and optical disks.

**Disk/Diskette Drive.** A unit used to read data from or write data onto one or more diskettes.

**Diskette.** A flexible, flat circular plate that is permanently housed in a black paper envelope. It stores data and software on its magnetic coating. Diskettes are often called floppy disks.

**Display Screen.** A device that provides a visual representation of data; a TV-like screen often called a monitor, cathode ray tube (CRT), or video display unit (VDU).

**Distributed Data Processing.** A computing approach in which an organization uses a number of computers located at a distance but connected to an office computer.

**Distributed Intelligence.** An arrangement whereby terminals and peripheral equipment in a system possess a certain amount of intelligence and do some work, eliminating part of the main computer's burden.

**Distributed Processing.** A network system in which work is distributed among connected computers and processed by them.

**Distribution List.** A list that identifies a collection of members. The name of the distribution list serves as shorthand in addressing groups collectively.

**Documentation.** The training manual that explains a program.

**Dot-Matrix Printer**. A printer that forms characters from a two-dimensional array of dots. The greater the number of dots used to represent a character, the more legible it is.

**Double Density**. A special recording method for diskettes that allows them to store twice as much data as normal (single-density) diskettes.

**Down Loading**. Transferring a file or program from one computer to another computer.

**Downtime**. The period of time when a device is not operating.

**Draft-Quality Printer**. A printer, usually high-speed dot matrix, that produces characters that are very readable, but of less than typewriter quality. A draft-quality printer is used for printing internal documents, where type quality is not a major factor.

**Drive**. A peripheral device that holds a disk or diskette so that the computer can read data from and write data onto it.

**Dumb Terminal**. A terminal that consists of a keyboard and an output device such as a screen. A dumb terminal is used for simple input/output operations and generally has no intelligence of its own.

**Duplex**. *See* Full Duplex.

**EBCDIC (Extended Binary-Coded Decimal Interchange Code)**. A standard communications code consisting of an 8-bit coded character set. This code is used primarily by IBM mainframe computers.

**Electronic Blackboard**. The generic name for audiographic devices used to send writing over normal telephone lines. As the sender writes on a board, the writing appears at the distant location on a television monitor.

**Electronic Circuit**. A pathway or channel through which electricity flows.

**Electronic File Cabinet**. An electronic storage unit that files data in much the same way as a regular file cabinet. It has some distinct advantages: a great deal of information can be stored in a small area, accessed and changed quickly, organized more efficiently, and kept more securely.

**Electronic Handshake**. An arrangement whereby devices that transmit data can query receiving equipment regarding transmitting speeds, mode selection, line quality, and other conditions for the most compatible transmitting conditions.

**Electronic Industries Association (EIA)**. A standards organization located in Washington, DC, that specializes in the electrical and functional characteristics of interface equipment.

**Electronic Mail**. A system that allows memos or messages to be sent from one or more person(s) or electronic devices(s) to others.

**Emulator**. A program that allows a computer to imitate a different system. This enables different systems to use the same data and programs to achieve the same results, but at possibly different performance rates.

**End-to-End Connection**. A through and open channel, like a telephone connection when people are speaking.

**Ergonomics**. The science of human-machine interaction.

**Error Message**. Text displayed by the computer when an incorrect response is typed. It explains the problem and indicates what to do next.

**Expert System**. Advanced computer programming that relies on a large body of specialized knowledge to give information on a professional task. Expert systems, also known as knowledge-based systems, are used for high-level management or complex applications.

**Facsimile (Fax)**. A process of scanning text or graphic material whereby the image is converted into signals. The signals are transmitted by telephone to a compatible terminal which is able to produce a copy of the original material.

**Fanfold Paper**. A continuous sheet of paper folded accordion-style and separated by perforations. It is used for computer printouts.

**Field**. The smallest unit of information or data within a record.

**File**. A collection of logically related records or data. A file is the means by which data is stored on a disk or diskette so it can be used at a later time.

**Filename**. The sequence of alphanumeric characters assigned by a user to a file so it can be read by the computer and the user.

**File Organization**. A system that determines the physical placement of data on a mass storage device.

**Firmware**. Software placed permanently on a "Read-Only Memory" (ROM) chip within a computer. It cannot be lost if power goes down.

**Flaming**. Anger that is produced by an electronic message.

**Floppy Disk**. A flexible magnetic disk that looks like a small phonograph record. It is used for storing information. Such disks, also called diskettes, can be erased and reused.

**Font**. A device that prints or reproduces a specific typeface. *See also* Typeface.

**Foreground Processing**. Top-priority processing; it has priority over background (lower-priority) processing.

**Form Definition Software**. A software package that provides facilities to design a screen display including field protection and data verification.

**Formfeed**. A printer feature that automatically advances a roll of fanfold paper to the top of the next page or form when the printer has finished printing one page or form.

**FORTRAN (FORmula TRANslation)**. A widely used high-level programming language well suited to problems that can be expressed in terms of algebraic formulas. It is generally used in scientific applications.

**Freeze-Frame Transmission**. Transmission of high-quality, still-motion images, about one every 35 seconds. Also called slow-scan or still-frame teleconferencing.

**Frequency Division Multiplexing**. A modulation technique that divides the total capacity of a channel into specific frequency bands.

**Full-Duplex**. A method of communication between two computers that allows transmission in both directions at the same time.

**Full-Motion Video**. Continuous-motion television images that support interactive group communications.

**Function Key**. A key that causes a computer to perform a function (such as clearing the screen) or execute a program. On some personal computers, some function keys, such as HELP and DO, and all the arrow keys have predefined actions.

**Gateway**. A special node that interfaces two or more dissimilar networks and provides protocol translation between them.

**GIGO ("Garbage In, Garbage Out")**. Refers to the fact that the quality of the output depends on the quality of the input data.

**Global**. Pertaining to an operation that encompasses a complete area, such as a file, program, or database.

**Graphics**. The use of lines, charts, images, and figures to display information.

**Group**. An organizational unit within a computer conference.

**Half-Duplex (HDX)**. A network in which data can be transmitted in both directions, but in only one direction at a time. An example of a half-duplex system is a speakerphone, where it is necessary to press a button before speaking to or interrupting the other speaker.

**Handshaking**. An exchange of predetermined signals between two computerized devices. It allows each one to ascertain whether the other is present and ready to transmit or receive data.

**Hard Copy**. Output in a permanent form, usually on paper or paper tape.

**Hard Disk**. A nonflexible disk (such as a Winchester disk), more expensive than a diskette but capable of storing much more data.

**Hardware**. The physical equipment that makes up a computer system and permits information storage and transmission.

**Hardware Interfaces**. The plugs and cables that connect equipment components.

**Hard-Wired**. Describing a permanent physical connection between two points in an electrical circuit, or between two devices linked by a communication line. Personal computer local connections are typically hard-wired.

**Hash Key**. A key that acts like an address.

**Head**. A component of a disk drive that reads, writes, or erases data on a storage medium such as a diskette or disk.

**Help Service**. Information displayed on the video screen that explains how to use applications and system services.

**Hertz**. A unit of frequency equaling one cycle per second.

**Horizontal Scrolling**. Horizontal movement of text to access more characters than are shown on the screen.

**Host Computer**. The controlling computer in a multiple computer operation.

**Icon**. A graphic image often used in place of words. For example, a scissors may appear on a monitor next to a word that is being cut out of the text.

**Impact Printer**. A printer that forms characters on paper by striking an inked ribbon with a character-forming element.

**In Box**. A file for incoming mail.

**Incompatible Devices (Equipment)**. Devices that cannot interact effectively (communicate) with one another.

**Index**. An electronic table of contents stored in the computer to aid in the search for material on storage media.

**Information Management**. Evaluation and modeling that use information stored in a well-structured data system.

**Information Services**. Publicly accessible computer repositories for data, such as stock exchange prices or foreign currency exchange rates, and other databases.

**Instruction**. A command that tells the computer what operation to perform next.

**Integrated Circuit (IC)**. A complete electrical circuit on a single chip.

**Intelligent Terminal**. A terminal that is capable of processing information; many store and retrieve information on their own tapes, disks, and printers. An intelligent terminal can be adapted to communicate with various host computers simply by changing the protocol programmed into it.

**Interactive Computer**. A computer that is capable of carrying on a real-time dialogue with the user via a keyboard.

**Interactive Software Package**. A program that provides the user with commands with which to submit requests and exercise control over the execution of the program.

**Interface**. A hardware connection that provides an electronic pathway for signals, or software which enables information to be exchanged between programs. Keyboards interface people and processors.

**Internal Memory Capacity**. Maximum number of characters the internal memory of a system can hold.

**Inverse Video**. A reversal of foreground and background on a terminal display screen. White characters would be shown on black instead of the reverse.

**I/O (Input/Output) Devices**. Equipment that works with a processor to permit information to be entered or extracted. A keyboard and display screen are examples.

**IRC (International Record Carrier)**. A worldwide communications network like RCA Global Communications and ITT World Communications.

**ISO**. International Standards Organization

**ITU**. International Telecommunications Union, located in Geneva, Switzerland.

**Job**. A computer task (program), such as reading a disk or printing a file.

**K**. The symbol for the quantity 2 to the tenth power, or 1024. The K is uppercase to distinguish it from the Standard International Unit (a lowercase k) for "kilo," or 1,000.

**Keyboard**. Typewriter-like terminal keys used for data entry.

**Key System**. A small internal company telephone system without switching capabilities.

**Keyword**. A word used to characterize the content of a file, document, or message. Used in indexes of a file.

**Kilobyte (Kb)**. 1,024 bytes.

**Knowledge-Based Management System (KBMS)**. A system that

searches for, organizes, controls, increases, and updates an area of knowledge. KBMSs are part of expert systems.

**Knowledge Engineering**. Designing knowledge-based programs and expert systems.

**LAN**. *See* Local Area Network.

**Large-Scale Integration (LSI)**. The combination of about 1,000 to 10,000 circuits on a single chip. Typical examples of LSI circuits are memory chips, microprocessors, calculator chips, and watch chips.

**Leased Line**. A permanent dedicated point-to-point or multipoint telephone circuit used for transmitting voice or data signals. The line is leased from a long-distance telephone company (common carrier) such as AT&T, and can be conditioned to permit higher transmission speeds than a standard line. *See also* Voice Grade Line.

**LED (Light-Emitting Diode)**. A semiconductor diode that emits light when it is charged with electricity.

**Letter-Quality Printer**. A printer used to produce final copies of documents. It produces typing comparable to that of a high-quality office typewriter.

**Light Pen**. A device that allows data to be entered or altered on a CRT screen.

**Line Printer**. A high-speed printer that produces an entire line of characters at one time.

**Line Speed**. *See* Data Communications.

**List Processing**. The word processing application that permits many copies of a form document to be produced with certain information changing from one copy to the next (e.g., the production of personalized form letters).

**Local**. Hard-wired connection of one computer to another computer, terminal, or peripheral device such as in a local area network.

**Local Area Network (LAN)**. A communications network connecting computer terminals and other devices within an organization. LANs may also connect with other private or public networks.

**LSI**. *See* Large-Scale Integration.

**Machine Language**. Information and instructions that can be used directly by the computer.

**Magnetic Tape (Magtape)**. Tape used as a mass storage media, and packaged on reels. Since the data stored on magnetic tape can only be accessed serially, it is not practical for use with personal computers, but it is often used as a back-up device on larger computer systems.

**Mail Database**. A depository of currently pending mail.

**Mailname**. User identification which is unique within a group, possibly the center, or even the system.

**Mail Qualifier**. An attribute of information in an EM system. Examples: Recipient; Sender; Forwarding permission; Copy permission; Special mailcode; Request for response; Site ID; Modification capability; Keep capability.

**Mainframe**. Centralized computer facility (CPU and main memory). It may delegate some of its work load to specialized processors.

**Mass Storage**. A device such as a disk or magtape that can store large amounts of data readily accessible to the central processing unit.

**Matrix Management**. Organization of work around work groups.

**Mbyte (MB)**. One million bytes, or 1,048,576.

**Medium**. The physical substance upon which data is recorded. Magnetic disks, magnetic tape, and punched cards are examples.

**Meet-Me Bridge**. A dial-up audio conferencing system. All conferees dial the same number and are connected together.

**Member**. A participant in a system.

**Memory**. (1) The main high-speed storage area in a computer where instructions for a program being run are temporarily kept. (2) A device in which data can be stored and from which it can later be retrieved.

**Menu**. A list of choices available to a user that is presented on a monitor. The user selects an action to be performed by typing a letter or by positioning the cursor.

**Menu-Driven**. Characterizing a computer system that depends primarily on menus rather than a command language for its directions.

**Message Switching**. Routing data toward its destination. This is done by the computer processor.

**Microcomputer**. Sometimes called a personal computer (PC) or small business computer. Micros usually support one user but, with increased power, may provide processing for several terminals. Physically very small, PCs fit on or under a desk. Microcomputer technology is based on large-scale integration (LSI) circuitry. Micros are usually the least expensive of the computer types.

**Micrographics**. Photographic processes by which information can be reduced to a microform medium and be stored and retrieved for reference.

**Microprocessor**. A single-chip central processing unit incorporating LSI technology. It performs the basic data processing functions of a computer.

**Microwave Transmission**. Electromagnetic transmission of data, audio, or video signals through open space on a line-of-sight path.

**Migration Path**. A series of alternatives outlined by a computer manufacturer that enable the user to introduce new computer equipment into a system. It allows an individual to increase a system's computing power by adding or trading components, rather than giving up current hardware and software.

**Minicomputer**. A type of computer that is usually smaller in size and capability than a mainframe. Its performance generally exceeds that of a microcomputer. Since minicomputers are more modular than mainframes, they can be configured to provide better price/performance systems.

**Mnemonics**. (1) Groups of letters and numbers that bring material (files or fields of information) onto a display screen. (2) Short, easy-to-remember names or abbreviations. Many commands in programming languages are mnemonics.

**Modem (MOdulator/DEModulator)**. A hardware device that permits computers and terminals to communicate with each other using analog circuits such as telephone lines. The modem's modulator translates the digital computer signals into analog signals that can be transmitted over a telephone line. The modem's demodulator converts analog signals into digital signals for the computer's use.

**Monitor File**. A file that will record all user activities for recovery and accounting purposes, as well as for recordable system errors.

**Monitor (Hardware)**. A television-like display screen that can be used as an output device. It is also called display screen, cathode ray tube (CRT), and video display terminal (VDT).

**Monitor (Software)**. Part of an operating system that allows the user to enter programs and data into the memory to run programs.

**MOS**. Metal-oxide semiconductor, the most common form of LSI technology.

**Multicopy Form**. A preprinted, multiple form that contains carbon paper between the pages (e.g., W2 forms and credit card receipts).

**Multidrop Lines**. A communication network in which more than one terminal is located on a single line connected to the computer.

**Multiplexer**. A device that combines streams of information into a composite signal and sends them along a communicating channel. A similar device reverses the process at the receiving end of a transmission.

**Multiprocessing**. Processing by two or more computers connected to run jobs concurrently for faster results.

**Multiprogramming**. A scheduling technique that allows more than one job to be executed at any one time. Thus, one CPU can appear to be running more than one program because it gives small slices of time for executing each program.

**Multitasking**. The execution of several tasks at the same time. Although computers can perform only one task at a time, the speed at which a computer operates makes it appear as though several tasks are being performed simultaneously.

**Nanosecond**. One billionth of a second.

**Narrowband Channel**. Usually refers to a telephone circuit that handles 3,000 hertz.

**Network, Electronic**. A group of computers or other devices connected by cables or through telephone lines. The computers send and receive data among themselves and share certain devices such as hard disks and printers.

**Node**. (1) Department of an organization. (2) A connecting point on a communicating network or between communicating channels.

**Nonsimultaneous Communication**. Receipt and transmittal of messages at a terminal regardless of whether a recipient is present.

**Nonvolatile Memory**. Memory that is not lost when a processor's power supply is shut off or disrupted.

**OCC (Other Common Carrier)**. Term originally used to describe telephone service companies other than AT&T. OCC now includes AT&T.

**OCR**. *See* Optical Character Recognition System.

**OEM (Original Equipment Manufacturer)**. A business that buys computer equipment from hardware and software manufacturers or vendors, and resells or repackages it.

**Off-Line**. Disconnected from a processor. Some off-line equipment can operate independently or in non-real time.

**OJT**. On-the-job training.

**On-Line**. Controlled directly in real time by the central processing unit. *Compare* Off-Line.

**Operating System**. Computer program that allows a computer to supervise its own operations. It accomplishes such functions as input/output control, memory allocation, and program read-in. Small systems are called monitors, supervisors, or executive programs, e.g., UNIX.

**Optical Character Recognition (OCR) System**. A light-sensitive optical scanning system that senses and encodes into digital format alphanumeric characters.

**Optical Disk**. Computer storage (memory) disk having potential for far greater capacity than a magnetic disk. Some optical disks can be re-recorded.

**Option Module**. An add-on printed-circuit module that allows expansion of a system. *See also* Board.

**Organizational Directory**. A directory of a computer conferencing system that contains information relating to its members, centers, and groups.

**Out Box**. A file or directory containing references to information distributed by a member.

**Output**. Information produced as a result of processing input data.

**Packet Switching**. A relatively new form of digital communication in which data bits are grouped into bursts (or packets) of fixed length so they can share a channel with other such bursts. When received at the destination, the bursts are separated and sent to the appropriate recipients.

**Parallel Communication**. Data transmission in which a number of bits are transmitted simultaneously over separate wires.

**Parallel Interface**. A feature allowing two lanes of data to flow simultaneously along a channel.

**Parallel Transmission**. Sending more than one bit at a time.

**Parameter**. A range of characteristics of a program/record or other area.

**Parity**. A "one-extra-bit" code used to detect recording or transmission errors.

**Parity Bit**. An extra bit added to a character's binary code to make it conform to the parity checking method. *See also* Parity Check.

**Parity Check**. A method of error detection in data communications that checks whether the sum of the 1 bits in each character received is even or odd. In odd parity, the sum of 1 bits in a character must be odd; if the character's pattern would otherwise be an even number of bits, it is transmitted with the added parity bit set to 1. In even parity, the opposite occurs; the parity bit is set to 1 for characters with odd bit patterns.

**Password**. A word each user may attach to his/her mailname. Passwords may also be attached to groups and centers for security purposes.

**PBX (Private Branch Exchange)**. An organization's internal switchboard.

**PCM**. Depending on the reference, either Plug-Compatible Manufacturer or Pulse Code Modulation.

**Peripheral**. A device that is external, but connected, to the CPU and main memory, e.g., a printer, modem, or terminal.

**Personal Computer**. *See* Microcomputer.

**Pixel (Picture Element)**. A dot or cluster of dots that forms the smallest unit of a picture that is seen on a computer display screen. For graphics displays, screens with more pixels generally provide higher resolution.

**Plotter.** A graphic drawing device.

**Point-to-Point.** Place-to-place or station-to-station.

**Polling.** A method used in data communications networks in which each terminal is asked if there is data to be sent.

**Port.** An input and/or output socket on a computer that is used to connect hardware such as modems or cables.

**Power Supply.** A transistor switch that converts AC power into DC power. It energizes components such as integrated circuits, monitors, and keyboards, and steps down the power supplied to some components.

**Printer.** Equipment that produces a paper copy of a document (hard copy output). There are impact and nonimpact printers.

**Printhead.** The element in a printer that forms a printed character.

**Printout.** Computer-generated hard copy.

**Printout Queuing.** A computer function that allows a number of documents to be lined up for printout. Some systems allow the operator to designate the order; others operate on a first-in/first-out basis.

**Processor.** The controlling unit or processing part of the computer system that reads, interprets, and executes instructions.

**Program.** The complete sequence of instructions and routines needed to solve a problem or to execute directions in a computer.

**Program Disk.** A disk containing the instructions for a program.

**Programming Language.** The words, mnemonics, and/or symbols, along with the specific rules allowed in constructing computer programs. Some examples are BASIC, FORTRAN, and COBOL.

**PROM (Programmable Read-Only Memory).** A permanent memory chip for program storage.

**Protocol.** A set of rules and conventions governing the formats used in data communications.

**Protocol Converter.** Device for translating codes or protocols between networks or devices.

**Public Data Network (PDN).** A packet- or circuit-switched network available to many clients. A PDN may offer value-added services at a reduced cost because of communications resource sharing. It also usually provides greater reliability as a result of built-in redundancy.

**Query Capability.** Commands provided for the user to select and retrieve information.

**RAM (Random Access Memory)**. Memory that can be read and written into (i.e., altered) during normal operation. RAM is the type of memory used in most computers to store the instructions of programs that are being run.

**Raster**. A computer graphics coding system. The coding represents the dots that compose a picture.

**Real Time**. The actual time an event is occurring—a term used to describe an on-line interactive application. Some computer conferences can be held in real time.

**Record**. A collection of related data items.

**Remote Job Entry (RJE)**. Entering jobs in a batch processing system at a location distant from the central computer site.

**Remote Terminal**. Input/output equipment attached to a system through a transmission network.

**Reprographics**. Mass reproduction of documents, graphics, and film by such processes as offset printing, photocopying, and microfilming.

**Resolution**. The degree of detail that can be seen on a display screen.

**Resource Directory**. An electronic file containing information associated with all private and public permanent storage areas within a computer conference.

**Reverse Video**. The ability to reverse a standard display on a terminal monitor to highlight characters, words, or lines.

**Ring Network**. A circular local area network in which messages pass from station to station by passing an access token or by means of a polling technique.

**RJ11**. A standard modular telephone jack into which a direct-connect modem can be plugged.

**RJE**. *See* Remote Job Entry.

**ROM (Read-Only Memory)**. Permanent memory written during manufacture, or a permanent memory chip for program storage.

**RS-232C**. A standard connection for serial computer communications as described by the Electronics Industry Association (EIA). The standard specifies the physical connections between computers and other devices, such as modems and printers, and defines characteristics (such as baud rate) of the electrical signals sent through the connection.

**Screen Editor**. A feature that supports the cursor concept. The cursor may be navigated around the display screen identifying portions of text to be manipulated. Line and character modifications are initiated by special character combinations, and blocks are manipulated by entering commands.

**Screen Format**. An arrangement of characters, numbers, or lines and columns that fill a screen.

**Screen Size and Type**. The dimensions and kind of screen display (CRT, gas plasma, or LED). A display screen facilitates the job of entering and editing text.

**SDLC (Synchronous Data Link Control)**. A transmission method in which data is gathered into blocks. Similar to BISYNC except that SDLC uses data bits to signal control functions instead of full characters. It is part of IBM network architecture.

**Search Capability**. The methods by which a system searches for an editing point. A system can search by document, page, paragraph, word, or character string.

**Serial Communication**. Data transmission in which each bit is sent separately and sequentially.

**Serial Interface**. A single-channel connection between computers and peripheral drives, printers, and modems.

**Serial Printer**. *See* Daisy Wheel Printer.

**Shared User**. A computer system that shares computer resources.

**Soft Copy**. Information presented on a display screen or in audio format, rather than as printed copy.

**Soft Disk**. *See* Diskette.

**Soft Keys**. Keys on a computer keyboard that can be given special functions or programmed to suit the user's needs.

**Software**. Instructions that make a computer perform a specific task or program.

**Software Interface**. A program that controls the way a computer program interacts with other programs it uses.

**Sort**. Rearranging information that has been filed in fields.

**Sort Keys**. Keys that indicate a sequence of information order.

**Speakerphone**. An amplified telephone that allows hands-free usage.

**Standard Member**. A member of a computer conference who participates in the system without having a leadership role.

**Star Network**. A network in which all equipment radiates from a central computer at the hub.

**Storage Media Capacity**. Maximum number of characters the storage media, such as magnetic cards, disks, or tapes, can hold.

**Storage Media Standard**. The design of disks and tapes used to store memory.

**String**. Alphanumeric data that is treated as a unit.

**Subject**. A one-line header used as a summary of the information content of a message, note, or document.

**Subroutine**. A group of instructions which are used several times in a program and can be called up as needed.

**Switched Line**. A type of data communications line used to connect computers over a telephone network.

**Synchronous Transmission**. A method of high-speed transmission in which the timing of each bit of data is precisely controlled.

**System Center**. A center established during the initiation phase of the system that will exist during its lifetime.

**System Components**. The physical parts of a system, such as a keyboard, CRT display, minicomputer, magnetic card reader or floppy disk drive, and printing device.

**System Security**. Methods used to prevent unauthorized access. Some systems provide an electronic key lock. A few systems have security codes so that only certain persons may have access to any stored document; this can be valuable if documents are being processed which should have restricted staff access.


**Tape Drive**. The I/O unit housing a magnetic tape reel that reads data recorded on tape and records data on the tape.

**Teleconferencing**. *See* Computer Teleconferencing.

**Teleprocessing**. Processing of data that is received from or sent to remote locations over telecommunication lines.

**Telex, TWX**. Switched telecommunication services.

**Term Dictionary**. A file or macro that stores a technical vocabulary of frequently used words and phrases that are specific to the individual business. They are retrieved by typing fewer characters than would normally be necessary.

**Terminal, Data Communication**. A terminal used in a data communications system for transmitting and receiving data.

**Text Editor**. A program that assists in text preparation and editing.

**Tie Line**. A voice or circuit trunk line between two PBXs.

**Time Division Multiplexing**. A method by which each node is allotted a small time interval during which it can transmit a message or part of a message. In this way, messages of many channels are interleaved for transmission. They are then arranged in their proper order at the receiving end.

**Time-Sharing Operating System**. A system that executes a number of processes at the same time though they are controlled from several different terminals.

**Token Passing System**. A method by which equipment waiting to transmit a message monitors a system, waits for an empty "token" or frame, and inserts a message and its address. When equipment finds a message addressed to it, it retrieves the message and sets the token on empty.

**Transceiver.** A device that both transmits and receives analog or digital signals.

**Transducer.** A device that converts sound waves to electrical signals.

**Transfer Rate.** The volume of information per time unit that gets transferred between a random access storage device and main memory, or between any two devices.

**Transparent.** Pertaining to any function that is invisible to a user.

**Typeface.** A specific style of print, including alphabet, numbers, and symbols, reproduced by a "font."

**Unlisted Member.** A member of a computer conference who experiences all the benefits of participating in the system without his/her participation being publicly known.

**Uploading.** Shifting information from memory banks of one computer to another, generally from a PC to another computer.

**User Interface.** The pathway or connection between a person and a device.

**Value-Added Carriers.** Communications networks that provide additional services.

**VAN.** Value-added network.

**Vertical Scrolling.** Vertical movement of characters on a display screen that allows more lines to be shown.

**Videotext.** A service that uses part or all of a TV screen for information displays called pages or frames. The information could range from weather or news to advertising for various services.

**Virtual Storage.** A method in which portions of a program are placed in auxiliary storage until needed. This gives the illusion of unlimited main storage.

**VLSI (Very Large Scale Integration).** Refers to micro-electronic chips carrying up to 1,000,000 transistors.

**Voice Grade Line.** A normal telephone line designed for voice communication.

**Voice Mail.** A system that provides computer-controlled deposit, storage, and delivery of voice messages.

**Voice Switching.** A systems feature whereby a speaker's voice activates a transmission.

**Volatile Memory.** Memory that is lost when the processor's power supply is shut off.

**WAN.** *See* Wide Area Network.

**Wide Area Network (WAN).** External dedicated or nondedicated, switched or nonswitched communications network.

**Winchester Disk**. A hard disk for computer memory storage.

**Word Processing**. Using terminal and related storage devices for data storage, manipulation, and processing needed to prepare letters and reports.

**Word Wraparound**. A feature of some equipment that automatically places a word on the next line when it cannot fit on the line being typed.

**Workspace**. A dedicated main memory storage area maintained by the system for each user during a session.

**Work Window**. Compartment on a monitor that displays work or documents. About six windows can be viewed at one time.

**X.25**. A protocol standard for interface connections between equipment and public data networks.

**X.400 Message Handling Facility**. A standard that would enable people using various communicating equipment and networks to exchange voice, text, and graphics messages.

# Bibliography

Adler, R. P., and Lipinsky, H. M. "HUB: A Computer-Based Communication System." In *Studies of Computer-Mediated Communications Systems: A Synthesis of the Findings*, Final Report to the National Science Foundation (S. R. Hiltz and E. B. Kerr, eds.), pp. 436-447. Newark, NJ: Computerized Conferencing and Communications Center, 1981.

Barney, Clifford. "Computer Conferencing with EIES." *PC Magazine*, vol. 1, no. 9, 1983, pp. 270, 272, 275.

Cross, T. B. *Virtual Management—Integrated Computer/Communications Management Systems*, pp. 51-63. London: Pergamon Press, 1980.

———. *Personal Versus Corporate Computing—Virtual Management*. Presented at the Pergamon Infotech SOAR Conference, London, 1981.

———. "Teleconferencing Revolution." *Colorado Business*, 1982.

———. "Computer Teleconferencing—Being There Without Going There." *Telecommunications*, 1982.

———. "Vertical Versus Lateral Thinking Systems." *Online*, January 1982, p. 6.

———. "Teleconferencing Can Reduce the Need for Travel." *The Office*, April 1982.

———. "Using Computer Conferencing in Telecommunications Management." *Business Communications Review*, May-June 1982, pp. 25-30.

———. "Telecos Offer Enhanced Services on the Road to Higher Revenues." *Telephony*, August 2, 1982.

———. "Computer Conferencing via Portable Terminals Solves Many Business Communication Problems." *Marketing News*, November 26, 1982, sec. 2, p. 12.

———. "Confusion in Store for PBX Mart of the Future." *Computerworld* (Special Report), January 31, 1983, p. 9.

———. "It's Time to Get Out of the Bleachers and Onto the Field of Computer Conferencing." *Communications News*, February 1983, p. 76.

**207**

Cross, T. B. "Computer Conferences: Beyond Electronic Mail." *Telcoms,* February/March 1983, p. 2.

———. "Virtual Management—Thoughts on a Virtual World." *Interface,* March 1983, p. 295.

———. "The Grapefruit Diet." *Journal of Micrographics,* April 1983, p. 14.

———. "Computer Teleconferencing: The Meeting That Keeps on Meeting." *Training,* May 1983, p. 76.

———. "The Future of the PBX: Promises and Problems." *Telephony,* May 2, 1983, p. 84.

———. "Getting Started in Teleconferencing." *Business Communications Review,* September-October 1983, p. 14.

———. "Teleconferencing Without Losing the Human Touch." *Words,* January 1984, pp. 16-19.

———. "Smart Buildings Next on Horizon." *MIS Week,* April 4, 1984, p. 39.

———. "Telecommuting—The Next Frontier." *MIS Week,* May 30, 1984, p. 38.

———. "Computer Conferencing." *ComputerWorld on Communications,* August 1, 1984, pp. 37-39.

———. "Electronic Mail: What Is It, Really?" *Teleconnect,* October 1984, pp. 80-81.

Didsbury, Howard F., Jr. (ed.). *Communications and the Future Prospects: Promises and Problems.* Bethesda, MD: World Future Society, 1982.

Feigenbaum, Edward A., and McCorduck, Pamela. *The Fifth Generation: Artificial Intelligence and Japan's Computer Challenge to the World.* Reading, MA: Addison-Wesley, 1983.

Ferguson, J. A. "PLANET: A Computer Conferencing System and Its Evaluation Through a Case Study." *Behavioral Research Methods and Instrumentation,* vol. 9(2), 1977, pp. 92-95.

Hiltz, S. R., and Turoff, M. *Electronic Networks: The Social Dynamics of a New Communications Medium.* Presented at the Annual Meeting of the American Sociological Association, San Francisco, 1978.

———. *The Network Nation—Human Communication via Computer.* Reading, MA: Addison-Wesley, 1978.

———. *Office Augmentation Systems: The Case for Evolutionary Design.* Presented at the 15th Hawaii International Conference on System Sciences, Honolulu, 1981.

Hiltz, S. R.; Johnson, K.; and Agle, G. *Replicating Bales' Problem-Solving Experiments on a Computerized Conference: A Pilot Study,* Research

Report No. 8. Newark, NJ: Computerized Conferencing and Communications Center, 1978.

Hiltz, S. R.; Johnson, K.; and Turoff, M. *The Quality of Group Decision Making in Face-to-Face Versus Computerized Conferences.* Presented at the Annual Meeting of the American Sociological Association, Toronto, 1981.

Hollerbach, Lew. *A 60-Minute Guide to Microcomputers.* Englewood Cliffs, NJ: Prentice-Hall, 1981.

Johansen, Robert; Vallee, Jacques; and Spangler, Kathleen. *Electronic Meetings: Technical Alternatives and Social Choices.* Institute for the Future, Menlo Park, CA. Reading, MA: Addison-Wesley, 1979.

Johnson-Lenz, P., and Johnson-Lenz, T. *The Evolution of a Tailored Communications Structure: The Topics Systems*, Research Report No 14. Newark, NJ: Computerized Conferencing and Communication Center, 1981.

Kalba, Konrad K., et al. *Electronic Message Systems: The Technological, Market and Regulatory Prospects.* Cambridge: Center for Policy Alternatives, Massachusetts Institute of Technology, 1978.

Keen, Peter G. W., and Scott Morton, Michael S. *Decision Support Systems: An Organizational Perspective.* Reading, MA: Addison-Wesley, 1978.

Kerr, E. B. "Conferencing via Computer: Evaluation of Computer-assisted Planning and Management for the White House Conference on Library and Information Services." In *Information for the 1980s: A Final Report of the White House Conference on Library and Information Services*, pp. 767-805. Washington, DC: U.S. Govt. Printing Office, 1979.

Kerr, E. B., and Hiltz, S. R. *Computer-Mediated Communication Systems—Status and Evaluation.* New York: Academic Press, 1982.

Kimberley, Paul. *Micro-Processors: An Introduction.* New York: McGraw-Hill, 1982.

Masuda, Yoneji. *The Information Society as Post Industrial Society.* Tokyo: Institute for the Information Society, 1980.

McAndrews, R. A. *Computer Teleconferencing Executive Training.* Presentation at the Second Annual International Tele/conferencing Symposium, Boulder, CO, 1982.

_____. *Computer Teleconferencing: What We Have Learned.* Presentation at the Third Annual International Tele/conferencing Symposium, Boulder, CO, 1983.

McQuillan, J. M. "A Retrospective on Electronic Mail." *SIGOA Newsletter* 1, pp. 8-9.

Martin, J. *Design of Man-Computer Dialogues.* Englewood Cliffs, NJ: Prentice-Hall, 1973.

Palme, J. *A Human-Computer Interface for Noncomputer Specialists,* FOA Report C 10128-M3(E5, H9). Stockholm: Swedish National Defense Research Institute, 1979.

———. *Experience with the Use of the COM Computerized Conferencing System,* FOA Report C 10166E-M6(H9). Stockholm: Swedish National Defense Research Institute, 1981.

Scher, J. M. "Higher Educational and Managerial-Organizational Uses of Computer-Based Human Communication Systems: Some Futures and Opportunities." In *Through the 80s: Thinking Globally, Acting Locally* (F. Festher, ed.), pp. 317-322. Washington, DC: World Future Society, 1980.

Steinfield, Charles. "The Nature of Electronic Mail Usage in Organizations: Purposes and Dimensions of Use." Abstract presented to International Communications Association. University Park, Houston: School of Communication, University of Houston, May 1984.

Turoff, M. "Delphi Conferencing: Computer Conferencing with Anonymity." *Technology Forecasting and Social Change,* vol. 3, 1972, pp. 159-204.

———. " 'Party-Line' and 'Discussion' Computerized Conferencing Systems." In *Computer Communication—Impacts and Implications* (S. Winkler, ed.), pp. 161-170. International Conference on Computer Communication, Washington, DC, 1972.

———. "The Designer's View." In *Electronic Communication: Technology and Impacts* (M. M. Henderson and M. J. MacNaughton, eds.), AAAS Sel. Symp. 52, pp. 113-120. Boulder, CO: Westview Press, 1980.

———. *Management Issues in Human Communications via Computer.* Presented at the Stanford Conference on Office Automation, Stanford, CA, 1980.

Turoff, M., and Hiltz, S. R. *Information and Communication in International Affairs.* Presented at the International Studies Association, Toronto, 1979.

Uhlig, R. D.; Farber, D. J.; and Bair, J. H. *The Office of the Future: Communication and Computers.* Amsterdam: North Holland, 1979.

Vallee, J. *There Ain't No User Science—A Tongue-in-Cheek Discussion of Interactive Systems.* ASIS Annual Meeting 13, 1976.

———. "Modeling as a Communication Process: Computer Conferencing Offers New Perspectives." *Technological Forecasting and Societal Change,* vol. 10, 1977, pp. 391-400.

———. "Computer Conferencing: The Management Issues." *Bulletin of the ASIS,* June 1978, pp. 17-19.

_____. *Confessions of a Computer Scientist.* Berkeley, CA: And/Or Press, Inc., 1982.

_____. "The Computer Grapevine." *Science Digest,* vol. 91, February 1983, p. 36.

_____. "Sitting In on a Computer Conference." *PC Magazine,* vol. 1, no. 9, 1983, pp. 256-257, 259.

Vallee, J., and Askevold, G. "Geological Applications of Network Conferencing: Current Experiments with the FORUM System." In *Computer Networks and Chemistry* (P. Lykos, ed.), pp. 53-65. Chicago: American Chemical Society, 1975.

Vallee, J., and Beebe, R. *TOPICS and NOTEPAD: New Management Tools for the Disseminated Task Force.* Presented at the National Telecommunications Conference, IEEE, June 1977.

Vallee, J.; Lipinski, H.; and Miller, R. *Group Communication Through Computers,* vol. 1. Menlo Park, CA: Institute for the Future, 1974.

Vallee, J., et al. *Group Communication Through Computers,* vol. 2. Menlo Park, CA: Institute for the Future, 1974.

_____. *Group Communication Through Computers,* vol. 3 and vol. 4. Menlo Park, CA: Institute for the Future, 1975.

_____. *Bulletin of the ASIS,* vol. 4, June 1978, p. 17-20.

# Index

## More Computer Books from
## Scott, Foresman and Company

## Order Form

**Send me:**

_____ Connections: Telecommunicating on a Budget, $14.95, 18159

_____ Local Area Networks, $17.95, 18064

_____ Guide to Telecommunications, $39.95, 15944

☐ **Check here for a free catalog**

**Please check method of payment**

☐ Check/Money Order     ☐ MasterCard     ☐ Visa

Amount Enclosed $_____

Credit Card No. _____

Expiration Date _____

Signature_____

Name (please print) _____

Address_____

City _____State_____Zip _____

Add applicable sales tax, plus 6% of the total for U.P.S.

Full payment must accompany your order. Offer good in U.S. only.

A18008